SECOND EDITION

THE J GIRLS GUIDE

The Young Jewish Woman's Essential Survival Guide for Growing Up Jewish

Penina Adelman, Ali Feldman and Shulamit Reinharz

REVISED, UPDATED AND EXPANDED BY

ELLEN GOLUB

For People of All Faiths, All Backgrounds

JEWISH LIGHTS Publishing

Jewish Lights Publishing
an imprint of Turner Publishing Company
Nashville, Tennessee
New York, New York
www.jewishlights.com
www.turnerpublishing.com

The JGirl's Guide:
The Young Jewish Woman's Handbook for Coming of Age
Second Edition

For information regarding permission to reprint material from this book, please write or fax your request to Turner Publishing, Permissions Department, at 4507 Charlotte Avenue, Suite 100, Nashville, Tennessee 37209, (615) 255-2665, fax (615) 255-5081, or email your request to submissions@turnerpublishing.com.

The Library of Congress has cataloged the earlier edition as follows:
Library of Congress Cataloging-in-Publication Data
Adelman, Penina V. (Penina Villenchik)
The Jgirl's guide : the young Jewish woman's handbook for coming of age / Penina Adelman, Ali Feldman, and Shulamit Reinharz.
p. cm.
Includes bibliographical references.
ISBN-13: 978-1-58023-215-9 (quality pbk.)
ISBN-10: 1-58023-215-9 (quality pbk.)
1. Jewish girls—Conduct of life—Juvenile literature. 2. Jewish girls—Religious life—Juvenile literature. 3. Coming of age—Juvenile literature. I. Feldman, Ali. II. Reinharz, Shulamit. III. Title.
BM727.A33 2005
296.7'0835'2—dc22
2005001674
9781580238533

17 18 19 20   10 9 8 7 6 5 4 3 2 1

Manufactured in the United States of America

Cover Design: Maddie Cothren
Interior Design: Tim Holtz

CONTENTS

Preface

BEING A J GIRL

I am a professor, a daughter, a mother, a sister, a wife, an aunt, a friend, and many other things. I'm also a JGirl—and probably you are, too. You can be a JGirl as soon as you're born and stay at it your whole life. You can become a JGirl later. Everybody's story is different.

Being a JGirl means thinking about the fact that you are Jewish and wanting to find out more about other Jews. It means getting excited when you discover that a competitor at the Olympics is a young Jewish person and wondering how she lives her life. It means wanting to check out the Jewish community if you travel to another country. It means reading the newspaper or surfing online with a special eye for what is going on in Israel or Jewish communities in other countries. It means trying to understand how you fit into that diverse community we call "the Jewish People."

The JGirl's Guide is for girls who have always been JGirls and for those who want to become JGirls. It's for learning what it takes to become one. It's written with you in mind.

MY STORY

I started on my JGirl path from the minute I was born in a Catholic hospital in Amsterdam, Holland. Both my parents had escaped from Germany as teenagers when the Nazis gained power. They thought they would be safe in Holland, but after they arrived there, the Nazis invaded that country as well. My parents (who were actually only boyfriend and girl-friend at the time) decided to hide rather than give up, just like Anne Frank did with her family. Unlike Anne Frank, how-ever, the people who would become my parents were never caught. Thus, when the war was finally over and the Jews could come out of their hiding places, my parents married, and nine months later I was born. With a history like that and with my parents giving me a Hebrew name—Shulamit—I was off and running as a JGirl.

Later, when we moved to the United States, I started going to public school during the day and Hebrew school on two after-noons and Sunday mornings. Unlike some kids, I loved it. It was great to learn a new language and be able to be a leader in Junior Congregation. Each time we participated in Junior Con-gregation, a star was put on a chart. I was pretty ambitious and loved getting those stars.

PREPARING TO BECOME A BAT MITZVAH

Then one day I turned 12 and it was time to start preparing for my bat mitzvah. Life was very different then from the way it is now. I sat with a teacher who gave me a recording (cer-tainly not an MP3) to learn my Haftarah (הפטרה). That was pretty much my entire training. Girls didn't do as much for their bat mitzvah ceremonies in the 1950s, when I had mine, as they do now. In those days, many girls didn't even become bat mitzvah at all.

During the summer in which I turned 12, my mother, baby brother, and I traveled to Israel to visit relatives and see the country. By ship it took two weeks to get there and two weeks to get back—with lots of seasickness along the way. I returned from Israel a very enthusiastic JGirl. Israel was 10 years old, and I was 12. I had lots of adventures in the *moshav* (rural town) I visited, including riding horses, building and sitting around campfires, and hanging out with Israeli kids. I loved everything Israeli. So when the movie *Exodus* came out, I went to see it and, of course, fell in love with that, too. I decided then and there that I would try to marry someone who shared the same ideas I did.

LIFE GOES ON

When I was 15 and living in a New Jersey suburb, I met an Israeli boy who had just moved to the United States. We became friends right away because he hadn't learned English yet, and I had learned enough Hebrew in Hebrew school and from my trip to Israel that we could communicate. After we graduated from college, we married, and later we had two daughters. We gave them Hebrew names (Yael and Naomi). They too became JGirls.

As a professor at Brandeis University in Waltham, Massachusetts, I teach sociology and women's studies. Many of the topics I study relate to issues that were important to me growing up. In 1997, I created a special research center to examine issues central to Jews and to women (the Hadassah-Brandeis Institute). Each summer we invite a few highly talented college students to work with us as interns. That's how this book, *The JGirl's Guide,* was born.

AND NOW THIS BOOK ...

One of the interns was Ali Feldman, a young woman from Toronto who came to work with us on new ideas she was developing for bat mitzvah girls. By the end of the summer, Ali had finished the first draft of a huge book on the topic. The next summer, she returned to continue her work, and I recommended that she contact Penina Adelman, a local professional who had a bat mitzvah–age daughter of her own and had run groups for mothers and daughters. Since then Penina, Ali, and I have worked hard to turn that first draft into a book of manageable size that girls can use wherever they live.

The story of this book doesn't end there. It became very popular among JGirls and bat mitzvah groups and went into several printings. But now, after more than ten years, we thought the book could use a refresh. Enter Ellen Golub, another JGirl, a professor, a writer, a mom and bat mitzvah coach. Ellen brought a fresh eye to the manuscript, updating and adding content and transforming this edition for the digital age and its generation of readers. You are now about to read the new and improved *JGirls Guide.*

Why did we spend so much effort preparing this book for you? The reasons are simple.

No matter how much has been written about being a Jewish girl, there is always need for more, because the lives of Jewish teens are constantly changing. When I was growing up, the TV was black-and-white and had only three channels. There were no iPhones, videos, DVDs, Internet, Facebook, or texting. Most middle-class suburban families had only one car; most moms didn't work outside the home. Hebrew day schools were very rare. Fewer JGirls grew up in divorced families, with single moms or stepparents, than is true today. More JGirls now than earlier grow up in families with two moms or two dads or in families where one parent may not be Jewish. Because life is changing so quickly, it is even more important to think about what it means to be a JGirl today.

A second reason we worked on this book is that some Jewish girls grow up in places where there aren't many Jewish kids. That was true for me. I didn't have many other Jewish girls to talk to, so I really could have used this book. However, no one wrote it for me, so we decided to write this for you. Enjoy!

—Shulamit Reinharz

How This Book Works

How do you go from being a girl to being a young woman with so many choices and challenges before you? You have more ways to know what's happening in the world, to contact people around the world, and to make your presence felt in the world than any other generation before you. You have more career paths open to you than your grandmother and maybe even your mother did. Could your grandmother have become an astronaut, a surgeon, a rabbi, or a construction worker? Could your mother have done that while having a family? You are more accepting than previous generations of alternative lifestyles, homosexuality, transgender, single parenthood, adoption, divorce, blended families, interracial relations, and other things that used to make people feel very uncomfortable. You have more choices about motherhood, from not having children at all to being a stay-at-home mom, and everything in between. How do you know which decision to make?

Add the Jewish factor and your life just became even more complicated. What does it mean to be Jewish today, let alone to be a Jewish woman?

Your body will take care of your physically becoming a woman, but your physical self still needs help from your mind, heart, and spirit. Where are the models for how to be a Jewish woman today? The public bat mitzvah ceremony is not even a century old—not a very long time in the span of 3,500 years of Jewish history. How did Jewish girls become women in the days of the Bible? How did they become women in the 19th century? How will *you* become a Jewish woman?

The JGirl's Guide is written for you. It will give you information, resources, options, and questions that you can think about on your own or discuss with girls your age. With the world becoming an increasingly complex place, this book can help you navigate your journey toward becoming a Jewish woman.

Language

A very important aspect of *The JGirl's Guide* is language. According to the Torah (תורה), the world was created with words. "God said, 'Let there be light,' and there was light" (Genesis 1:3).

Perhaps that is why words and language are a cornerstone of Judaism. Over the centuries many commentaries have been written to further explain the words in the Bible. No word's meaning is taken for granted.

We have already used a few words that have very complicated meanings and may mean different things, depending on whom you ask. For example, *God, Judaism, Jewish,* and *the People Israel* mean one thing to a Reform Jew and another thing to an Orthodox Jew. Other examples of words that may not mean the same things to everybody are *matriarchy, patriarchy, feminist, girlfriend, boyfriend, family, partner, convert,* and *marriage.*

We have taken great care in choosing the words we use in *The JGirl's Guide.* Even so, we may unintentionally use words that make you feel left out or confused. It can be painful for someone who does not live with their parents to keep hearing about families where children always live with a mother and a father. Similarly, girls with health problems may be made uncomfortable by discussion of "a healthy body," a phrase they might not feel applies to them. If we use words that make you feel like an outsider, we apologize. That certainly wasn't our intention. What words would you use instead?

For example, take the word *God.* Did you wonder who or what *God* was when you were a small child? What do you think *God* means now? Has the meaning changed for you over the years? Do you think it could change again? Do you like to use Hebrew words for God, other words altogether, or no words at all?

Hebrew

Now a word about Hebrew and how we use it in this book. Hebrew is the language of the Bible and the language of the State of Israel and of many Jewish people today. It is the language that ties Jews together wherever we live. It is also, especially, the traditional language of prayer and includes many words and sentence structures that do not translate well into English. For example, in the biblical story of Creation, the name of the first human being is Adam. This word comes from the Hebrew root Alef-Dalet-Mem (א–ד–ם), which means "earth" or "ground." What the name Adam really means is "earthling," which makes sense because Adam was made out of earth. You would never know that from the English, however.

Because Hebrew is such an important vessel for the content of Jewish life, we have provided the Hebrew spelling for words and concepts when they first appear, transliterated or translated into English. Whether you know Hebrew or not, you will thus have the opportunity to the see the word on the page in its original incarnation. We hope you will look for and recognize these words again along your JGirl journey. The founder of Hasidism, Israel Baal Shem Tov, believed that since the universe was created by God speaking it into existence, all things were ultimately created through the combination of the Hebrew alphabet's 22 letters.

The Bible

This book will contain many references to the Bible, which is the most important book in Jewish tradition. When Jews are called the People of the Book, the Bible is the book in question. The Bible includes a number of smaller books, like the Book of Esther. When reference is made to a passage from the Bible, the name of the book is given along with the number of the relevant chapter and verse within that book. The story of the creation of light, for instance, appears in Genesis 1:3—that is, the third verse of the first chapter of the first book of the Bible.

The first books of the Bible are called the Five Books of Moses: Genesis (called *Bereshit*–בראשית–in Hebrew), Exodus (*Shmot*–שמות), Leviticus (*Vayikra*–ויקרא), Numbers (*Bamidbar*–במדבר), and Deuteronomy (*D'varim*–דברים). These five books are also called the Torah, as is a handwritten scroll that contains these books. The Hebrew Bible, or Tanakh, also contains the works of the prophets and other writings such as Job, the Book of Ruth, and Chronicles. The word *Tanakh* (תנ״ך) comes from the first letter of the Hebrew words *Torah* (Instruction–תורה), *Nevi'im* (Prophets–נביאים), and *K'tuvim* (Writings–כתובים). The Hebrew Bible is what Christians call the Old Testament. At the end of this book there is a glossary of Hebrew terms that will help you to understand Judaism better. You can skip over them or learn them. Judaism is very much tied to the Hebrew language, so we suggest you try to learn some Hebrew. If you already know a little Hebrew, we suggest you learn more.

Activities

In each chapter there are different sections that focus on an array of activities, skills, and Jewish knowledge. Following is a list of the different types of sections you will encounter. (These do not always appear in the order that they are listed here.)

Learn

In this section you will find the background and explanation of the *mitzvah* or *mitzvot* associated with each chapter. Included are ancient and modern Jewish sources, as well as current material from psychology, sociology, anthropology, and folklore to deepen your understanding. You will also learn Jewish concepts like *kol k'vodah bat melekh p'nimah,* which we will discuss in the next chapter. These aren't *mitzvot*. They are values that guide Jewish practice and life. Remember: a mitzvah is something that you DO!

m'korot מקורות (Jewish sources)

These are quotes and excerpts from ancient and contemporary Jewish sources that we hope you will use as inspiration for reflection and discussion.

Here is an example from an eighth-century commentary on the Book of Ecclesiastes in the Bible. Talking about the challenge of finding words of truth, the author of Ecclesiastes compares "words of the wise" to "nails well driven in" and "spurs" that poke an animal to make it move. The commentary, however, makes a surprising and very different comparison. It says:

> The words of the wise are like a young girl's ball. As a ball is tossed by hand without falling, so Moses received the Torah at Sinai and delivered it to Joshua, Joshua to the elders, the elders to the prophets, and the prophets delivered it to the Great Synagogue. —*Kohelet Rabbah* 12:11, on Ecclesiastes 12:11

What do you think of this comparison? What does it say about the commentary's view of young girls?

Discuss

In this section we encourage you to ask questions and form opinions. If you are reading the book with a group, you can explore your ideas together. Much of Jewish thought has been developed through discussion. In rabbinic times, sages (smart Jewish men) argued and reasoned over the meanings of Jewish texts in pairs or small groups called chavruta (חברותא). We invite you to delve into the ideas in this book and make them your own.

Meet

Here we introduce you to Jewish women from all walks of life, all ages, all nationalities, and all backgrounds. Some are famous. Some could be your next-door neighbors or friends.

Write

Writing, particularly journal writing and blogging, have been ways for girls and women to document their lives, confess secrets that could not be spoken anywhere else, and talk about sensitive issues like physical changes, relationships, and sexuality. There is rich material everywhere for writing, even in the routines of daily living.

Since 1947, reading *The Diary of Anne Frank* has been a profound experience in self-affirmation for Jewish girls around the world. In her diary, Anne Frank presents the daily and inner life of a girl hiding from the Nazis in Amsterdam during the Holocaust. She wrote each entry beginning, "Dear Kitty," as if it were a letter to her best friend. You might like to try addressing a fictional or real friend of yours.

We encourage you to keep a journal or blog as you read this book. Writing a journal can help you clarify your goals and priorities, figure out your relationships, and learn more about yourself. In "Write," we offer you exercises for writing and using a journal. That way you can have an ongoing dialogue with the book and read what you have written to see how your ideas and viewpoints may have changed from the beginning of the book to the end.

Here is an exercise to warm you up. Think of something you wanted to do ever since you were a little girl but were always told, "You're too young. Wait until you grow up." Write about it or draw it in your journal. If you're into video, do a video selfie with your phone. Don't forget to save it!

Pirkei Banot

The title of this section is adapted from the title of a famous book of wisdom called *Pirkei Avot,* which means "Sayings of the Fathers." In *Pirkei Banot,* which means "Sayings of the Daughters," we offer you quotes from girls and women, Jewish and non-Jewish, across the ages. Here is one by Jewish feminist Gloria Steinem: "Each others' lives are our best textbooks."

Do It

This section suggests ways you can put into action the things you've learned about in each chapter. You've become familiar with the *mitzvot* described in the chapter; now it's up to you to experience them for yourself!

Think about It

These are additional points to consider about the topic in question, whether on your own, talking to a friend, or in a discussion with a larger group.

Resources

If you want to know more about a particular subject mentioned in *The JGirls Guide,* check out the "Resources" section in the back, offering you a selection of books and websites that you can turn to for more information.

Introduction

*I'm a Jewish girl and so I'll
become a Jewish woman—is there
any more to it than that?*

Welcome—ברוכים הבאים—
FROM THE AUTHORS

Dear JGirl,
Welcome to The JGirl's Guide, *a book for you to read and experiment with and share with your friends. And congrats on your coming of age as a JGirl! We know that bat mitzvahs often come with gifts, great food, and lots of dancing—and that the celebration can sometimes overshadow the Jewish experience. Of course, a bat mitzvah is more than a giant birthday party. It is your formal induction into the community of Jewish sisterhood. How can this event connect with your life and become truly meaningful? How can it speak to your issues and launch you into the lifelong experience of being a JWoman? Good questions! We wrote this book— and solicited ideas from girls your age– to provide some answers.*

JGIRLS SPEAK

Dear JGirl,

I've been giving feedback on this book for quite a while. I'm 13, and I live in Livingston, New Jersey. I like reading, singing, music, writing, animals, helping others, and being with my family. Working on The JGirl's Guide *was great because my opinion counted for something. I love writing, so I enjoyed putting my thoughts down on paper—actually, in the computer. Growing up is a tough time for all girls. I think a book like this can make the teenage years less stressful.*

Yours,
  Ariela

Dear JGirl,

Hi, I'm Emily or Leah Malka, whichever you prefer. I'm 11, and I live in Holliston, Massachusetts. I love reading and writing long stories, making scrapbooks, and drawing. I also play the piano. I'm interested in large families, multiple births, and the McCaughey septuplets (seven babies born at once). I know, that's a strange interest!

I enjoyed writing for The JGirl's Guide *because as I answered the questions that were posed I was able to think about what I believe about certain subjects. In my opinion, only girls can truly relate to and understand what other girls are thinking and experiencing. It was awesome to be able to share my thoughts on topics relevant to our lives as teenage girls!*

Happy reading!
  Emily

Dear JGirl,

My parents and grandparents were Conservative Jews, so I had my bat mitzvah in the Conservative synagogue to which we belonged. In the summers I attended a Zionist camp. My grandparents were Holocaust survivors, so I became interested in finding out more about my roots and heritage.

After my bat mitzvah, I had the feeling that I had missed an important opportunity to pause before I went from being a Jewish girl to a young Jewish woman. Something was missing, but I didn't know what. I never spoke about it. My parents would have been disappointed. My teachers would not have understood. My friends would not have been interested—at least, that's how I felt.

Later, in the first week of high school I was offered my first cigarette, a kiss from a boy, and pressure to join one group of friends over another. It would have been great to have a book, a person, or a resource to turn to that spoke my language and tackled head-on the issues I was facing. That's why I got involved in The JGirl's Guide.

Greetings from California,
Ali

Dear JGirl,

I'm 21 and a senior in college focusing on American civilization and Hispanic studies. My hobbies include learning new things and exploring new cultures, traveling, hanging out and going out with friends, watching movies, listening to music and going to concerts, dancing for fun, and taking part in Jewish and Hispanic culture.

I loved being part of this book. It was really fun to be able to revisit my adolescence and all the issues and concerns I had to deal with at that time. Through books and diaries and pictures,

I was able to look back at my own coming of age—at the person I was then and the person I am now—and use that knowledge to try to help Jewish girls who are going through the same thing across the country. I know something like it would have been very helpful to me. Have fun and good luck—in adolescence and beyond!

Yours truly,
 Naomi

A Royal Daughter, a JGirl

Who are you? It is rare that we set aside time in our lives to think about who we really are, what makes us unique, and what we want in life. *But Judaism offers us the bat mitzvah year to do just that.* We are all a combination of many forces and influences, such as our families, the media, the music we like, our friends, and the activities we do in our free time. Finding out who we are at our core is a tough task.

One saying that Judaism offers to discover who we are is a favorite of ours. It's not some elaborate math equation or physics formula that requires intense analytical thinking. It is a phrase from Psalms: *Kol k'vodah bat melekh p'nimah* (כל כבודה בת מלך פנימה), which can be translated as "The true majesty of a royal daughter is inside her" (Psalm 45:14). In modern terms, this means that it's OK to feel great about yourself—to feel majestic, even—and to listen to your inner self.

In several Jewish sources, Jewish women are considered to be "daughters of a king," the king being God. Some people are uncomfortable equating God with a king because a king is an authoritarian male figure. However, this is only one way of describing God. God is also described as a Warrior, a Father, a Compassionate One—even a Nursing Mother. When the Torah describes God in human terms—as royalty, for example—it gives us a useful metaphor closer to our own experience. When we think of ourselves as "royal daughters" we use a metaphor that may help us to explore what feeling like royalty can mean.

Perhaps when we discover our inner selves and let our inner voices direct our lives, we become majestic and magnificent. Becoming "a royal daughter" doesn't necessarily mean being adorned with jewels and lavish clothing. It means relating to an inner self that may not always feel whole or bursting with self-esteem, but in whom these things are potential. It means loving who we are inside, appreciating our unique characteristics, and allowing our internal voice to guide our lives. This theme of *Kol k'vodah bat melekh p'nimah* (כל כבודה בת מלך פנימה) will appear throughout *The JGirl's Guide.*

WHO IS A JEW?

There are many different definitions of a Jew. Some people define Jews as people who believe in the Jewish religion—but many Jews who may not believe in God still live Jewish lives.

Who is a Jew and what is a Jewish life? Am I Jewish because I have a specific belief system or because I carry out rituals or behave in a certain way? Jews come from many different countries and cultures, so our customs can differ widely. According to Orthodox and Conservative Judaism, you are Jewish if you are born to a Jewish mother. According to Reform and Reconstructionist Judaism, you are Jewish if you have a Jewish father (even without a Jewish mother) and are raised as a Jew. A Jew can also be a person who converts to Judaism, like Ruth in the Bible, whom you'll read about in the chapter on friendship. Some people call converts "Jews by choice," but according to Jewish tradition they are Jews, the same as those who are born Jewish, and not to be treated any differently. It has even been noted that in American culture, where assimilation is often so easy and enticing, we are all Jews "by choice"!

WHAT DO ALL JEWS SHARE?

Jews are called "the People of the Book" because we gave the world the Torah and have spent thousands of years interpreting it. In addition to the Torah, we created the Talmud, one of the fundamental texts of Judaism. One of the most striking aspects of the Talmud is that it is a conversation among hundreds of people over the generations debating and telling stories about Jewish life and law. When a legal issue is being debated, all opinions about the topic are included, even those that disagree with the majority opinion. *The JGirl's Guide* is like the Talmud in this respect. We present many opinions, viewpoints, and ways of living a Jewish life so that you can learn about the mosaic that is Judaism and make up your own mind about how to be a Jew. This book will not try to change you into a very religious person, nor will it try to take you away from religion. It will not attempt to make you believe in something specific. Instead, we hope that *The JGirl's Guide* will help you to think about what being Jewish means to you. We firmly believe that Judaism can actually help you to deal with many issues you face today.

Coming of Age

Throughout the world and throughout time, girls have participated in rituals marking their "coming of age." A bat mitzvah belongs to this type of ritual. It marks the passage from child to adult, from girl to woman within the family and community. It is a beginning, not an end. In some coming-of-age rituals, such as the Navaho *Kinaalda,* a girl is believed to become the goddess of fertility and life. Her tribe treats her afterwards as one who holds the power of bringing life into the world.

The Upanayana, or Sacred Thread Ceremony of the Hindu people in India, has been revived in the last 35 years for girls. Now girls as well as boys learn the sacred teachings of their culture and receive a three-stranded thread symbolizing their coming of age. Many communities in Nigeria practice the Fattening Ceremony, in which unmarried girls prepare for womanhood by eating starchy foods and sleeping a lot. This way they embody the ideal woman, someone who is fat and symbolizes health, wealth, and beauty.

As a bat mitzvah girl, you do not become a goddess. However, you do become filled with the power of Jewish tradition. You embody all the wisdom of the Jewish People up until now. You can demonstrate this in many ways, for example, by learning Hebrew, reading Torah, leading prayers, giving a speech about your Torah portion, or doing good deeds on behalf of others. By taking on the responsibility of doing *mitzvot* (the plural of *mitzvah*)—or more *mitzvot* than you did before—you begin to take your place as a responsible Jewish adult and contribute to your community.

What's a Mitzvah? (מצוה)

Jewish tradition teaches that before the world was created, there was chaos and confusion. God created the world with the goal of establishing order and harmony. The world could run properly only when there were guidelines and strategies to structure it and keep it peaceful. According to tradition, that's why the concept of mitzvah was born.

Literally, the word *mitzvah* means a "commandment" given by God, and it refers to two sets of relationships, one between a person and God, and the other between one person and another. Though they may require effort or commitment, *mitzvot* actually help us to interact meaningfully and successfully with others, the world around us, and ourselves. In the language of the Jerusalem Talmud, a *mitzvah* can be a good deed, really any act of charity or service. In the language of the Babylonian Talmud, doing a *mitzvah* gives the sense of being connected, whether to God or other people, because a *mitzvah* is always an attempt at repairing and reorganizing an imperfect world.

The word *mitzvah* is also used more generally to mean "a good thing to do"—as in "It would be a real *mitzvah* to go over to the new girl sitting alone in the cafeteria and have lunch with her." This kind of *mitzvah* is specified in the Torah as an act of lovingkindness, treating a stranger well, loving your neighbor as yourself.

Mitzvot offer excellent advice on how to deal with every situation. They refine our sensitivities by telling us to think and study. But they also relate to ordinary tasks like walking the dog, helping with dinner, cleaning your room, and taking out the garbage. They include taking care of your body, being a great friend, and helping your sibling (if you have one) with homework. Believe it or not, the *mitzvot* can apply to practically all areas of your life. They are guiding principles steeped in ancient wisdom that are still relevant to modern people.

Each chapter in this book is linked to a specific *mitzvah* and concepts related to it. The Talmud tells us that there are 613 mitzvot: 248 positive ones—such as "Love your neighbor as yourself" (Leviticus 19:18)—and 365 negative ones—such as "Don't embarrass people" (Leviticus 19:17). Maimonides, who lived in the 12th century and is known as one of the greatest philosophers in Jewish history, listed these 613 *mitzvot* in his master work, *Sefer Hamitzvot* (ספר המצוות—The Book of *Mitzvot*), linking each one with its supporting reference in the Bible. Each of the *mitzvot* you will find in this book come from Maimonides' list.

According to the Talmud, a Jewish woman is given three specific *mitzvot* that are uniquely hers to perform: (1) lighting Shabbat candles, (2) baking Shabbat *challah* (חלה—special Shabbat bread), and (3) when married, observing the laws of family purity by bathing in a *mikvah* (מקוה) each month, after her period. Some Jewish women choose to do these and others do not. Some of the more general *mitzvot* deal with ethical issues that are obviously important, such as honoring your parents or taking care of orphans and widows. Some refer to details of behavior that might not *seem* important, like separating a piece of dough from the *challah* before baking it. Not all of the traditional *mitzvot* are possible to do today, even by the most observant person, because they were activities done at the Temple in Jerusalem, which was destroyed 2,000 years ago. Other *mitzvot* can be done only if you live in Israel. Still, mitzvot are the essential tools that all Jews use and think about on a daily basis. As you use these tools, you become a bat mitzvah.

THE JGIRL'S GUIDE: A FRESH PERSPECTIVE

The JGirl's Guide is a chance for you to see what practical advice and guidance Judaism has to offer as you journey through your adolescent years in our pop-culture world. Just as your body changes dramatically during your teen years, so does your personality and soul. In Judaism ages 12 and 13 are perceived as the beginning of maturity; that is why this is the traditional age of bat and bar mitzvah, respectively. Secular society also defines ages of maturity, when you are given the right to drive a car, to vote, to serve in the armed forces, and to drink alcohol.

Just as you can choose to get a driver's license or vote, you can choose to do *mitzvot*. Some Jews choose to follow the *mitzvot* because of their ethical nature, whereas other Jews choose to follow *mitzvot* because they feel good about the structure and discipline it gives to their lives. As a *bat mitzvah*, at whatever age, you can take on as many or as few *mitzvot* as you like. You are probably carrying out some of them already, simply in the way you live, but carrying out a *mitzvah* is even more rewarding if you know that you are doing it and why. The point of this book is to give you the information you need so you can make your own decisions about how you choose to be a Jew.

Whether you are about to become a *bat mitzvah* or have already done so; whether you do it formally in a synagogue with your family and community or quietly through your own Jewish study, *The JGirl's Guide* can give you a fresh perspective and lead you to consider ideas way beyond the notion that being a young Jewish woman today is cool, fun, meaningful, and personal. This book helps you to explore the relevant topics in your life and discover Jewish wisdom and guidance on these topics. Did you ever think that there might be Jewish sources or advice on how to deal with your first kiss? Pressure from your friends? Arguing with your parents? This book gives you an opportunity to see your Judaism, adolescence, and femininity combined, in order to become a Jewish woman in the most meaningful way possible.

A Few Historical Basics

If you've had a strong Jewish education, you probably already know the following facts about our history and traditions. If you haven't, this section will give you some background that will provide context for the rest of the chapters in this book.

Our religion originated approximately 3,500 years ago. It began with a few essential people, the 3 patriarchs and 4 matriarchs we learn about in the Bible: Abraham and Sarah, Isaac and Rebecca, and Jacob, Leah, and Rachel. Although the Talmud (Berachot 16b) lists only these seven as our spiritual ancestors, many modern Jews recognize two additional matriarchs, Bilcha and Zilpah, who each bore two sons to Jacob. Rachel and Leah, Bilcha and Zilpah, are remembered in the acronym Barzel (iron–ברז״ל), indicating the strength of the foremothers.

In biblical times we multiplied and became a nation of tribes. There were righteous characters and sinful ones, role models and villains. After a period of being enslaved in *Mitzrayim* (Egypt–מצרים), we wandered through the Sinai desert for 40 years until all the men who had fled Egypt died. Their wives, children, and grandchildren then settled in the Promised Land "flowing with milk and honey," the Land of Israel. In about 900 B.C.E., King Solomon built the First Temple in Jerusalem; it was the most prestigious, holy, and glamorous center for Jewish life. Nebuchadnezzar and his army destroyed the First Temple in 586 B.C.E., and the people were dispersed in the Babylonian Exile. Seventy years later many of the exiles returned, and rebuilt the Temple. The Second Temple stood for 600 years, until the Romans destroyed it in 70 A.C.E.

After that destruction, our religion adapted to life without a central place of worship—which continues until this day. The era of Torah and priests gave way to the rabbinic age. We established great councils of sages who studied the Bible and created books of interpretations and explanations of the Torah. Some of the famous sages of this period were Rabbi Akiva (ר' עקיבה), Rabbi Yochanan ben Zakkai (ר' יוחנן בן זכאי), and Rabbi Yehudah haNasi (ר' יהודה הנסיא). Amid the centers of study for men, there were also places where women were experts in Jewish law. Women such as Bruriah (ברוריה), Ima Shalom (אמא שלום), Yalta (יאלתה), and Rava's wife (אשת רבה), Rabbi Chisdah's (רב חסדא) unnamed daughter excelled in Torah learning and became authoritative voices in their communities. But because women were mostly confined to domestic tasks during premodern times, there were not nearly as many female sages as male. (What an opportunity for Jewish girls like you, now that Torah study is available to both sexes!)

THE RABBINIC AGE

The rabbinic age was a rich era filled with scholarship and study. Over several centuries, rabbis and great scholars composed two important works, the Mishnah (משנה) and the Gemara (גמרה). Together these two strands of rabbinic discussion form the Talmud and explain the Torah in a much more detailed way. These books were filled with pages of discussion and debate, including many disagreements and alternative opinions. The sages also developed creative explanations that filled in the gaps in Torah stories. This kind of creative explanation is known as Midrash (מדרש).

Later scholars continued the process of commentary and explanation, and the rules they established are the basis of traditional Judaism today. Some of the most famous sages were Rashi (רש״י 1040–1105), Maimonides (רמב״ם 1135–1204), Nachmanides (רמב״ן 1195–1270), and Rabbi Yosef Karo (יוסף קארו 1488–1575).

When the Second Temple was destroyed, the Jews were expelled from their land and forced to scatter throughout the world. Gradually they adopted some of the ways of the people and cultures surrounding them. Jews in Spain began speaking Spanish and formed their own Jewish-Spanish language called Ladino. They also began to integrate Spanish customs into their own practices. Jews in Germany began speaking a form of German that became known as Yiddish. Jews in Italy spoke Judeo-Italian and adopted some of the customs of that land. Jews whose customs developed from Spain and other Mediterranean countries became known as Sephardi (ספרדי), and Jews whose practices come from Germany, Russia, and eastern Europe became known as Ashkenazi (אשכנזי). Jews from Asia, Persia (Iran), and the Arab countries are sometimes called Mizrachi (מזרחי), or Oriental Jews. Ethiopian Jews, cut off from rabbinic Judaism, developed their own practices. Separated geographically, but devoted to understanding how to perform the *mitzvot* (מצוות) of the Torah, Sephardi and Ashkenazi Jews developed different rabbinic authorities. The Mizrachi rabbis wrote the Jerusalem Talmud (*Talmud Yerushalmi* תלמוד ירושלמי), and the Ashkenazim wrote the Babylonian Talmud (*Talmud Bavli* תלמוד בבלי). (Owing both to their similarity and to the expansion of the yeshiva educational system in Europe, the Bavli is the one most widely cited today.) It was once the case that Talmud was studied only by men, but modern times has opened that opportunity to women. There are now many female Talmud scholars, like Avital Hochstein and Judith Hauptman.

The study of Torah has been a Jewish passion throughout our history. It is one that continues today as rabbis, teachers, and students engage in being "detectives" of Torah. Today Torah learning is much more accessible and available to Jews throughout the world because of the printing press and the Internet. Every Shabbat morning, in synagogues throughout the world, there is an opportunity to learn Torah. There are literally thousands of books and online sites that offer and promote Jewish learning. (A list can be found at the end of this book.)

THE VARIETIES OF JEWISH EXPERIENCE

Over the centuries Jewish life has been filled with joys and sorrows. Sometimes Jewish communities grew and flourished; sometimes they experienced persecution, death, and destruction from their neighbors. As Jewish communities migrated into central and northern Europe, the Jewish Enlightenment emerged. The Enlightenment was an intellectual movement that swept across Europe in the 18th century. As Jews were finally permitted to become citizens of some of the countries in which they lived, many challenged traditionalists and decided to adopt a more secular, liberal, and open-minded way of life. As a result, the Reform movement was born in Germany, seeking ways for people to maintain a Jewish identity while assimilating into secular Christian cultures. In the United States this movement developed in two different directions: one became the contemporary Reform movement, and the other became the Conservative movement, which evolved as a backlash against Reform's extreme assimilationist changes (like not wearing kippot and holding services on Sunday, rather than Shabbat). The

Reconstructionist movement, which broke off from Conservative Judaism to emphasize Jewishness as a culture, developed in the mid-20th century. While some movements adopted the more liberal ideas of the Western world, another movement evolved that tried to uphold strict adherence to Jewish law while being actively involved in the modern world. Modern Orthodoxy emphasized a commitment to the strictness of Jewish law, such as how one dresses, prays, and eats, but also encouraged an involvement in the secular studies, professions, and cultures.

New groupings of Jews and Jewish life are always being added and refined. You will hear words like *Haredim* (הרדים) for ultra-Orthodox Jews and *secular* or *humanist* used for Jews with only cultural—not religious—affiliations. You may have even heard people you know saying they are "*Jew-ish*," referring to a having a Jewish style.

Owing to a very long period in diaspora, we have become a numerically small but varied people living in every country on earth. Jewish history can be seen as a roller coaster, filled with highs and lows. There are loops of progress, through scholarship, spirituality, and practice, and there are loops of destruction, filled with anti-Semitism, expulsion, and wandering. The roller coaster continues—with the majority of world Jewry now living in the United States and Israel! So now you have a brief overview of Jewish history.

Ahavat Yisrael
(Love of the People Israel)

JGirls come in many shapes and sizes with diverse backgrounds, practices, and ideologies. Some wear tank tops and miniskirts. Others wear long skirts and long-sleeved shirts. Others wear jeans. On Friday nights and Saturday mornings, some JGirls go to synagogue while others go to *shul* and still others hang out with friends, play soccer, do their homework, or just sleep late.

Some JGirls celebrate holidays with family and friends while others spend time in synagogue praying. Some JGirls do all these things and some do very few.

One reason we wrote this book is that we love all Jews! This is actually a *mitzvah* known as *ahavat Yisrael* (אהבת ישראל—love of the Jewish People). When you love someone, you don't think about whether that person belongs to this group or that group; whether they make their hot chocolate in a pan on the stove or in a mug in the microwave; or whether they prefer watching a sunset or a sunrise. You love that person for who he or she is inside. We welcome and embrace differences in the pages of this book and we hope that after you read it, you will have a greater sense of love, respect, and tolerance for your fellow JGirls.

In *The JGirl's Guide,* you will meet a variety of JGirls, each unique in her own way. There is a midrash that states that all Jews, even those not yet born, were at Mount Sinai to receive the Torah. The midrash goes on to say that each one of them had his or her own interpretation of the Torah. One beautiful thing about Judaism is that it leaves room for each individual to find their own Torah within the Torah we all share and within the practice of Jewish life. Judaism is colorful and multi-textured like the special coat of Joseph, whose story is told in the Book of Genesis.

One thing we would like you to take away from this book is *ahavat Yisrael,* love and respect for your people. Although there is often disagreement about practice and belief in Judaism, the special bond within the Jewish community around the world is very important because, as the Talmud says, we are all responsible, one for another (*Kol Yisrael arevim zeh bazeh* כל ישראל ערבים זה בזה). We hope to create space within these pages for all JGirls to unite over their common experience of entering into the Jewish People.

Mitzvah מצווה:
Ve'ahavta l'reyakha kamokha (Love your neighbor as yourself)
ואהבתה לרעך כמוכה

Learn לימוד:
Brit (covenant, mutual commitment) ברית
G'milut chasadim (acts of lovingkindness) גמילות חסדים
T'shuvah (repentance, saying you're sorry and will try to do better)
תשובה

Being a Friend

*I love my friends, but it's hard
to be a really good friend.*

Dear JGirl,

Friends rock!

Who do you hang out with in school at lunchtime? Who helps you to choose the best clothes at the mall? Who lends you a book she loved the minute she finishes it? Who do you text with?

Your friends are the coolest people in your life these days. They may hang out with you at lunch, after school, and on weekends. You may text with them daily—or maybe you prefer to play soccer or tennis with them. Whatever you do, friends—both girls and boys—are probably a major part of your life.

Friends may also help you to deal with questions about relationships, dating, discomfort with your changing body, and fights with your parents. They are there to stick up for you when others gang up on you and to share some chocolate if you get a bad grade or are not chosen for something you want.

Sometimes, though, friendship can get messed up. Your friends may do things that really upset you, like breaking promises, ignoring you, or telling your secrets. They may demand too much of your time or cancel plans with you to be with someone else. Teen friendship seems to include at least some fighting, frustration, and even fury! Sometimes your negative feelings may pass. Sometimes you may realize that your best friend really isn't your best friend. Sometimes you may ask yourself, "What's the point of friends, anyway?"

This chapter will get you thinking about what it means to be a good friend and how to make your friendships even better.
Ali

What Are Friends?

People define friendship differently, but all definitions have certain things in common: trust, loyalty, care, respect, understanding, similar values and shared interests, enjoying time together, and feeling comfortable around each other. In this chapter you will learn about being a good friend. You'll also get to know some famous friends in the Bible and make comparisons with your own friends. You'll come up with the essential ingredients of a good friendship, and you'll be able to test these.

One interpretation of the *mitzvah ve'ahavta l'reyakha kamokha* (love your neighbor as yourself, Leviticus 19:18) is that self-love is the basis of friendship. When you care enough about yourself, you make sure to stay healthy. You take care of your needs for love, mental stimulation, beauty, shelter, and understanding your place in the universe. You are a better friend when you are able to be good to yourself. Three aspects of the *mitzvah* of self-love are covenant, acts of lovingkindness, and repentance.

In Judaism the idea of a covenant, a contract between two responsible parties, is the foundation for a good friendship. In the Bible, God makes a covenant (Hebrew—*brit*) with the Jewish People, promising them the Land of Israel if they lived according to the Torah. Today, a covenant means that two or more people agree to do or not to do something specific. Friendship is a covenant between two or more people to be good friends, however they define it. It is also the delicious reward of a well-maintained relationship.

⬤ Discuss THE THREE SIGNS OF THE COVENANT

Here are three signs of covenant that occur in the Bible, followed by questions for you to think about and/or discuss.

- **Rainbow:** a sign of God's promise, made after the great flood in the story of Noah. The promise was never to bring destruction on the world again. "When I bring clouds over the earth, and the bow appears in the clouds, I will remember My covenant between Me and you and every living creature among all flesh, so that the waters shall never again become a flood to destroy all flesh" (Genesis 9:14–15).

  Question: When you and your friends get angry and frustrated with each other, can you find a way to fix things and renew your friendship? Can you appreciate the differences between you and your friends? Differences can actually enrich your relationship, even though it may be difficult to accept that you and your friends do not always think or feel the same way.

- **Shabbat:** a weekly reminder of the covenant between God and the Jewish People. "The Israelite people shall keep the Sabbath, observing the Sabbath throughout the ages as a covenant for all time: It shall be a sign for all time between Me and the people of Israel" (Exodus 31:16–17).

  Question: Do you and your friends have a way of reaffirming your friendship on a regular basis?

- **The Torah:** the collected wisdom and way of life of the Jewish People, a gift given by God. "If you listen to these laws and keep them and do them, *Adonai*, your God, will keep the covenant and the lovingkindness sworn to your ancestors" (Deuteronomy 7:12).

Question: Friendship is something you get, because you give. How do you understand this?

Pirkei Banot

"My friends know things about me without my having to tell them, just by my attitude and face. I can tell them anything and they're not going to judge me. I can't go for that long without talking to them. We know almost everything about each other." —Lauren, 15

"One of the most important characteristics [of a friendship] should be trust. A good friend must be trustworthy. They should care about you, love you, listen to you, help you mend a broken heart, share experiences with you. A good friend is considerate, is always there for you, and is someone you can count on. They should be nice, friendly, interesting, and supportive. There are so many things that make up a good friend, but a really important thing is loving you for who you are." —Ariela, 13

Do It Who Is Your Friend?

Write 10 points describing your friend. These can include name, favorite music, foods, activities, hobbies, and talents. Consider why you are friends and what you like most about this person.

Share your descriptions with your friend if you like.

meet David and Jonathan דוד ויהונתן

A sincere friendship is based on intimacy, privacy, honor, respect, giving and taking, and all-around care for one another. In the Bible, the story of David and Jonathan exemplifies the

Jewish ideal of friendship. Jonathan was the son of King Saul. When the king realized that David, a humble shepherd, was a far better warrior than he and was destined to be the next king of Israel instead of his own son, Jonathan, he became jealous and decided to kill David. Jonathan had to make a choice between his father and David, who was his friend. He sacrificed his relationship with his father and chose loyalty to his friend (1 Samuel 18:1–4). Jonathan helped David flee and thus saved his life.

What does it mean that they were such good friends? Did Jonathan call on David every 10 minutes? Did they spend all of their free time together? Did Jonathan constantly shower David with compliments? No. They were called good friends because they loved each other and would have done anything for one another. When he learned of Jonathan's death, David said, "I grieve for you my brother, Jonathan. You were most dear to me" (2 Samuel 1:26). Most friendships are not a matter of life and death, but in certain circumstances they can be.

◗ meet Naomi and Ruth נעמי ורות

In the biblical period of the Judges, there was a famine in Israel. One wealthy and prominent family in Bethlehem, from the tribe of Judah, was able to escape. Elimelech, his wife, Naomi, and his two sons, Chilion and Machlon, packed up and moved to the land of Moab, where there was food.

When they arrived in Moab, life improved. Elimelech continued with his business, Naomi was delighted in their new home, and the boys assimilated to their environments. Chilion married a Moabite woman named Ruth, and Machlon married a Moabite woman named Orpah. Life was good for Elimelech and his family: they had a large house, plenty of food, and good health.

Then things took a turn for the worse. Elimelech, Machlon, and Chilion died. Naomi's daughters-in-law remained with her throughout the period of mourning. Soon Naomi decided that it was time for her to return to her home in Bethlehem. At first both her daughters-in-law insisted that they would return with her, but when Naomi explained that she had nothing to offer them, Orpah went back to her own family in Moab.

Ruth, however, insisted on staying with her mother-in-law. When Naomi told Ruth she was free to go home, Ruth said, "Do not urge me to leave you, to go back from following you—for wherever you go, I will go; where you lodge, I will lodge. Your people are my people, and your God is my God. Where you will die, I will die, and there I will be buried" (Ruth 1:16–17).

It must have been very difficult for Ruth to leave her homeland and journey to another land with an entirely different religion and way of life. For Ruth was not only being loyal to Naomi. By saying, "Your people are my people and your God is my God," she became Jewish. For this commitment, Ruth has become a symbol of the convert in Judaism.

When they arrived in Bethlehem, a wealthy and kind landowner named Boaz, a cousin of Naomi, allowed Ruth to gather barley in his fields during the harvest. (This is a right guaranteed by the Torah to the poor, to widows, and to orphans.) Ruth worked in the sweltering sun every day, and one day Boaz invited her to eat with him. When Naomi noticed his growing interest in her daughter-in-law, she encouraged Ruth to let him know she was available for marriage.

Ruth did so, and Boaz and Ruth married and had a son named Oved, who became the grandfather of King David, the greatest king of Israel. According to Jewish tradition, Ruth and Boaz merited such a remarkable descendant because of their caring behavior, toward each other and toward others. A simple but beautiful explanation of the purpose of the Book of Ruth was given by Rabbi Zeira, who said: "This scroll tells us nothing either of ritual purity or impurity, either of things prohibited or permitted. Why then was it written? To teach how great is the reward of those who perform acts of kindness" (*Ruth Rabbah* 2:14).

Discuss

- Can you recall a time when you became friends with someone unexpectedly?

- Do you think girls have a different kind of friendship with girls than they have with boys? How so?

- How would you define loyalty? If a friend tells you a secret and you refrain from telling anyone, are you being loyal? If you hear someone speaking badly about your friend, can you still be a loyal friend if you don't speak up to defend her? If someone posts a negative comment or embarrassing photo of your friend online, should you tell your friend?

- What acts of kindness did Ruth and Jonathan perform? Can you think of a time in your own life when you acted like Ruth or Jonathan?

Learn

Ruth and Naomi and David and Jonathan exemplify a major pillar of Jewish belief, a concept called *g'milut chasadim*, which means doing acts of kindness. *Pirkei Avot* (1:2) says that the world rests on three things: (the study of) Torah, service (prayer) to God, and acts of lovingkindness. Examples of *g'milut chasadim* are welcoming guests into your home, helping someone in need, and greeting people kindly rather than harshly. Jewish tradition explains that just as God performs acts of kindness, so should we: "Blessed are You, God, who performs acts of lovingkindness," we say in the daily prayers.

A separate but related mitzvah is *bikkur cholim* (ביקור חולים), visiting the sick.

What is lovingkindness, and how do these two biblical pairs show us how to do it?

The Hebrew term for the quality of lovingkindness is *chesed* (חסד); performing acts of lovingkindness is *g'milut chasadim*.

Helping someone with no other motivation than being there for them is an example of *g'milut chasadim*. Ruth accompanied Naomi because she didn't want her mother-in-law to be alone and suffer. She put aside her own needs to be with her birth family, to remarry there and have children in her community. Jonathan put David's needs ahead of his own, even risking his life to save him.

Do you think acting as unselfishly as Ruth and Jonathan did is possible today?

Do you think it is possible to take care of oneself while being totally unselfish?

Do It Random Acts of *Chesed*

Sunday

- Offer to help a parent with chores around the house.
- Take flowers to a neighbor, friend, or relative.
- Smile at one person you don't know.
- Post a birthday greeting to a contact on Facebook.

Monday

- Wish a parent, sibling, bus driver, or friend at school a good morning.
- Call or text a grandparent, an aunt, an uncle, or a cousin to say hello.
- Recycle all the drink bottles and cans at your lunch table.
- Pick up a piece of litter and throw it away.

Tuesday

- Make your bed without being asked.
- Read a story to your younger sibling.
- Sit with the "new girl" at lunch.

Wednesday

- Thank your teacher for something during school.
- Send someone who is feeling sad a humorous tweet or email.
- Wish all the members of your household "sweet dreams."

Thursday

- Compliment your friend on an accomplishment.
- If someone was absent from school, text her and tell her the homework she missed.
- Bring your neighbor's recycling box back from the curb.

Friday

- Call a friend to wish her or him "Shabbat shalom."
- Water the plants in your house without being asked or reminded to do it.
- Set the table for dinner.

Saturday

- Take your younger sibling for a walk.
- Spend some time with a friend or relative who is sick, lonely, or depressed.
- Plan a special outing with a family member.

Pirkei Banot BE A MENSCH!

Menschlikhkeit, the quality of being a *mensch* (מענטש–Yiddish for "a good person"), is a "cousin" of the idea of *chesed*. This story from Itka Zygmuntowicz, who grew up in Poland and came to the United States in 1953, illustrates this principle. Itka was a prisoner in three concentration camps and the only person in her family to survive the Holocaust.

I remember once I came home crying bitterly because, as I was walking home from school, a group of non-Jewish kids I did not even know attacked me. When I came home, my mother asked me, "Why are you crying, Itka?" And I told her. She tried to comfort me. Later, she looked at me, and she asked me, "What did you do, my child?" And I said, "Nothing." And my mother said with assurance, "Well then, you have nothing to cry about.

Your *menschlikhkeit* does not depend on how others treat you but on how you treat others."

Discuss BEING A FRIEND

Use any of the following quotes that inspire you to start a discussion about friendship with a friend, parent, sibling, or classmate.

"Walking with a friend in the dark is better than walking alone in the light." —Helen Keller

"A person who loves a friend cannot stand by and watch that friend be beaten and insulted. The person would come to the friend's aid." —Rabbi Moshe Chaim Luzzato, *Mesilat Yesharim* 19:17

"Friendship is like a heart-flooding feeling that can happen to any two people who are caught up in the act of being themselves, and who like what they see." —Letty Cottin Pogrebin

"The greatest good you can do for another is not just to share your riches, but to reveal to him his own." —Benjamin Disraeli

Problems with Friends

Learn

The Hebrew word *t'shuvah* (תשובה) means "turning" or "turning back." It's what Jews do every Rosh Hashanah and Yom Kippur when we "turn" our attention back to the year that has just passed. Looking back on the year, we see things that we wish we had done differently, things we wish we had or hadn't said, things we would change in our behavior. We take stock and try to figure out how we might "turn the situation around" and do better next time. *T'shuvah* means the ability to feel shame and remorse for something we have done, to change our ways, to "turn back" after a quarrel or mistake and apologize to someone, asking for forgiveness (*slichah*–סליחה) and pardon (*m'chilah*–מחילה).

With a friend, there are always opportunities for *t'shuvah* because friendship is dynamic; it is always changing. This is the nature of human beings and their relationships. Sometimes we are both on the same wavelength; at other times we can hurt each other to the core. Friends, like all people, do not usually remain the same as time passes. If they did, the friendship could get pretty boring!

What Are the Arguments About?

Do these sound familiar? Look at this list and see how many of these friendship trouble spots ring true for you.

- Forgetting something important to the other person.
- Jealousy over possessions, other friends, grades, parents
- Divulging secrets
- Breaking plans
- Talking behind each other's back
- Lying to each other
- Asking one to lie for the other

Resolving Arguments

"One who covers a transgression seeks love, but one who repeats a matter separates close friends." —Proverbs 17:9

Arguments and disagreements with your friends don't necessarily signal the end of your friendship. In fact, how you handle a disagreement can be a valuable test of a friendship. Friends who are able to disagree about things and still be friends will be able to grow together. Some friendships, however, cannot withstand disagreement or differences of opinion, and these friends might need to go in different directions, or the relationship might need to change significantly.

Here are some tips on "making up" with your friends:

- Talking loudly or crying may prevent you from accurately conveying your feelings. Instead, try to speak in a calm voice. If you feel too upset to talk about it, you can always communicate your feelings in a letter or e-mail.

- If you have a problem with a specific person, confront that person directly and privately. This requires courage and has to be done with good manners, but you won't solve the problem unless you speak to the relevant person. Talking *about* someone to another only makes things worse. "Do not go talebearing among your people" (Leviticus 19:16).

- Always be specific as to why are you are upset and emphasize your own feelings. For example, "I felt embarrassed in front of the entire lunch table after what you said today!" Saying how you felt will release the anger. "You shall not take revenge or bear a grudge" (Leviticus 19:18).

- Listen and don't interrupt. If you want respect when you are talking, you must give the same respect to your friends. We know that's difficult.

- Attacking and name-calling are counterproductive; they will only prolong the argument and deepen hurt feelings.

- Don't tell others to dislike a former friend. You wouldn't want someone to do this to you.

Pirkei Banot SECRETS AND CLIQUES

"One of the most difficult friendship problems I've ever encountered is knowing when to tell a secret—when a friend is in trouble and confides in you, and you know you need to tell someone. Maybe she has an eating disorder and it endangers her health. It's so difficult to consciously break a friend's trust, even though you may know you're doing the right thing. But the most important thing to remember in a situation like that is: despite whatever anger your friend throws at you at the time, you're doing the right thing for her." —Rachel, 17

The Ins and Outs of Social Groups

Cliques are the underside of friendship. The dictionary defines *clique* as a "small, exclusive group of people." Everyone has had experience with a clique, either being in one or being left out of one. Human beings naturally form groups to accomplish tasks, to support each other, or to learn together. Your family is your first group experience. For better or worse, you are automatically included in your family when you are born or adopted.

Obviously, you are not born into your group of friends. Friendship is a matter of choice. People may come into and go from your group as they wish, or people may be allowed in one at a time and only if they fit certain requirements of the group.

People form cliques to gain a sense of control and power. Members of a clique can accept or reject new members. Sometimes, in order to feel better about themselves, members single out someone to reject. This is called *scapegoating*. The term comes from the Torah. In biblical times, the Israelites observed Yom Kippur by projecting their sins onto a goat that would then be sent into the wilderness—hence a "scapegoat." The people were then forgiven of the sins that they had put on this goat (Leviticus 16:9–10).

People come up with many "reasons" to scapegoat other human beings. As Jews, we should be extremely sensitive to this, because throughout history we have been scapegoated— for the death of Jesus, the Black Death (also called The Plague), and many other tragedies. We have been singled out, libeled, shunned, and degraded because people projected their own problems onto the Jews. The Anti-Defamation League (ADL) is an organization established over a hundred years ago to combat hate crimes against Jews. Even today, Israel and Jews worldwide have become the targets of violent political and religious movements that seek to defame and eliminate us. The Holocaust is the ultimate example of this cruel behavior to date, when scapegoating of Jews evolved into genocide.

Cliques use scapegoats to make it clear who is "in" the group and who is "out." Especially online, people can bully and marginalize others, while sometimes remaining anonymous. Under pressure to behave according to what is acceptable to the group, people often scapegoat others because they are "smart" or "stupid," "confident" or "too quiet," "good-looking" or "ugly." In the area of friendship, most of us have been guilty at one time or another of scapegoating others.

Learning how to handle life when you are included in or excluded from a group is a major step on the road to maturity. It can help to ask older siblings, cousins, parents, teachers, and coaches how they handled cliques.

❯ Think about It INSIDERS AND OUTCASTS

Take some time to think about these questions:

- How do you deal with the cliques you've encountered?
- What should you do if you hear someone putting down Jews or badmouthing Israel?
- Do you have a group of friends who hang out only with each other and no one else? If yes, how do you feel about being "inside" this group? How do you feel about those "outside" your group?
- Are you friendly with different types of people who do not belong to any one group? Why or why not?

Pirkei Banot

"I do not know what's wrong, but something is definitely wrong! I would like to know whether there are any other girls in this whole world like myself. I am anxious, crazy to learn, but at the same time want to go out and have a good time; true, I am not quite so crazy for the boys as the majority of girls are and when in company with them I am quite shy.... I am continually getting myself into embarrassing situations; embarrassing to myself alone, yet they bother me for 24 hours after." —Jennie Franklin, November 26, 1890

Write

This is a good time to use your journal or blog to explore what friendship means to you. Here are some questions and suggestions to start you thinking, but don't limit yourself to these ideas. Wherever your writing takes you will be valuable.

- What does friendship mean to you?
- What importance does friendship have in your life?
- Who is your oldest friend? How have you managed to stay friends so long?
- What do you look for in a friend now that is different from what you used to look for in a friend?
- Have you had a problem with a friend? How did you solve it?
- Write a poem about friendship.
- Write an email to a friend. (You may choose to show it to her or not.) Tell her what you appreciate about your friendship; tell her ways in which you would like to change your friendship.
- Would you like to make a new friend? What would that person be like? Do you know him or her already? Are you ready to try to become their friend? How can you make it happen?

Final Words

Now you know the three pillars of friendship, *brit, g'milut chasa-dim,* and *t'shuvah.* These pillars support you in your quest for meaningful, positive, healthy relationships. You have the tools to be a better friend, to yourself and to others. Consider this: You are your own best friend. No one will ever know you better than you know yourself. Because you are no longer a "little girl," you can take on the adult task of getting to know yourself. Being your own best friend will let you become a friend to others. In a story called "Happiness," Anne Frank wrote the following about one of her characters: "I haven't found happiness yet," she said, "but I found something else—someone who understands me."

Being a Daughter

*I love my parents,
but do I need to
honor them, too?*

Dear JGirl,

One minute they're making your lunch for school. The next, they're asking you to change your clothes and wear something more "appropriate." Later on they give you a kiss and wish you a nice day. Although they may let you go to the movies with your friends on the weekends, they insist on an early curfew, no negotiations.

Your relationship with your parents may be changing these days for a number of reasons. Not only do parents have to adjust to your new interests and energy (you are bursting with hormones, ideas, sexuality, peer pressure, and many other things), you are going to have to change as well, in order to meet them halfway. While you insist on a later curfew, more privacy, and boys in your room, they may insist on the opposite.

One of the most important mitzvot *is honoring your parents—in fact, it's so important, that it's one of the Ten Commandments (*aseret hadibrot–עשרת הדיברות). *How do you do this in a world that is telling you that parents are old-fashioned and overprotective, that parents can't understand you, that parents don't have a clue what life is about? Many parents went to school before there was an Internet and when standards for behavior were more conservative. Can they even understand the world you inhabit?*

The way you and your parents communicate these days may be more challenging than when you were younger and more dependent on them. You are changing, and they are learning to deal with your changes. One of the hardest things about becoming a teenager is learning how to adjust your relationship with your parents. Although you might still love them deeply, you might feel that they don't understand you or why you get frustrated with them. Yet you might also feel that you are growing closer with them and that your experience of the teen years is going fairly smoothly. The main thing is to keep talking about it all—together.

When you feel as though your parents don't understand you, remember that there is an age gap. They still see you as their baby girl, although you might see yourself as an independent person now. This struggle has been going on since parents and children have existed. You want more privacy, independence, and freedom. They want to let you have all these things, but they worry about your safety, your feelings, and your future.

Parents are also there to be your guides when the going gets tough. Remember, they too went through puberty, crushes, high school, and confusion! In this chapter there are suggestions on how to stay close to your parents and have a meaningful relationship with them while you all navigate the bumpy road to independence.

Good luck!

Ali

The Fifth Commandment

Learn

The commandment to honor your parents is taken very seriously in Judaism. The fifth of the Ten Commandments is *Kabed et avikha ve'et imekha* (Honor your father and your mother) (Exodus 20:12). The first five commandments all have to do with relations between God and humans; the second five have to do with relations between humans and humans. One might think that the command to honor one's parents would be part of the latter half, but it isn't. Honoring your parents is included in the first category because God is considered to be the third partner, with the parents, in making children. When you honor your parents, therefore, you also honor God (Babylonian Talmud, *Kiddushin* 30b and *Niddah* 31a). This is hard for young people to do, especially in an age of blended families and complex relationships. The Jerusalem Talmud (*Peah* 1:1) says, "Honoring a father and mother is the most difficult mitzvah."

Let's also consider what *parents* means. Today, there are traditional families that include a mother, a father, and children, and there are nontraditional families such as grandparents and children; single parents and children; adoptive parents and adoptive children; foster parents and foster children; stepfather, mother, and children; father, stepmother, and children; and same-sex parents and children. Whenever you see *parents* in this chapter, it means adults in the parental role, not necessarily the biological parents of the child. According to *halakhah* (Jewish law–הלכה), the legal code of traditional Judaism, people who assume a parental role with a child whose biological parents are not able to take care of him or her are to be honored just like biological parents.

Every form of Judaism considers the family unit to be essential in supporting the Jewish People. In traditional Judaism, parents are considered to be the earthly embodiment of what

God is to humans. As God is the Power that creates us, the Power to which we owe gratitude for our lives, so too are our parents in the earthly realm. If we dishonor our parents, we dishonor God, the Source of our existence.

Because you and your parents have different needs, it is crucial to search for ways to enable both of you to deal with change. As you progress from being a child to becoming an adult, you change the way you see your parents. As a child, you probably saw your parents mostly as providers and people who love you unconditionally. As an adult, you will be able to see them as people with strengths, weaknesses, and needs of their own. You will begin to recognize the respect and honor that they deserve.

As you are changing your view of your parents, they are changing their view of you. They will start to see you as an individual, someone who is still dependent on them yet learning how to be self-sufficient. In this chapter you will find ways to show your gratitude and appreciation.

Jewish Mothers

Meet *Ima* (Mother-אמא) and *Imahot* (Matriarchs-אמהות)

Each of us has a personal mother, a woman who gave birth to us and raised us. Some of us may have more than one mother—one who gave birth to us *and* one who raised us. Eve, the first mother on earth, was called *em kol chai* (אם כל חי—mother of all that is alive). As Jews, we also have four ancestral mothers, the women who gave birth to the Jewish People. They are Sarah, Rebecca, Rachel, and Leah. The Midrash and Feminist commentary sometimes include two other women—Bilhah and Zilpah, who were the wives of Jacob and the mothers of Jewish tribes—as well (see, e.g., *Numbers Rabbah* 12:17). The four wives of Jacob is a familiar acronym in Hebrew (Barzel-ברז״ל), which means "iron," using the first letter of each matriarch's name to allude to the power of these women in our tradition.

Here is a family tree of the matriarchs and patriarchs.

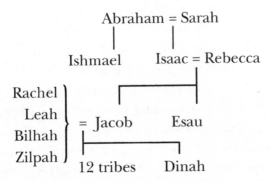

Following are descriptions of the four matriarchs. In Hebrew, the word for "matriarch" is the same as the word for biological mother, *ima.*

meet *Sarah Imeynu* (Sarah, Our Mother–שרה אמנו)

Sarah's name means "princess." She became the wife of Abraham, the founder of monotheism, although she was his brother's daughter, i.e. Abraham's niece. (Such marriages were common at the time.) Sarah went with Abraham on his mission to leave his birthplace and go to a new land to start a new people. Together they spread the message of One God.

Sarah is known for her beauty and speaking her mind and saying what bothered her. When she could not have a child, she told Abraham to have a child with their maid, Hagar, and "Abraham listened to the voice of Sarah" (Genesis 16:2). Hagar's child was named Ishmael, who today is considered the forerunner of the Muslim people, who appeared later, around the 7th century C.E.

Meanwhile, God finally promised Sarah, at age 90, a child. When she heard this, Sarah "laughed within herself, saying 'After I am grown old shall I have pleasure, my lord being old also?'" (Genesis 18:12). She gave birth to Isaac, who soon became his half-brother's rival. Sarah thought that Hagar was disrespectful to her, so she convinced Abraham to send Hagar and Ishmael off into the wilderness.

Later, Sarah woke up one morning to find that Abraham and Isaac had left the house early. At that moment Abraham, at God's command, was preparing to sacrifice his and Sarah's son on Mt. Moriah. In the end, however, an angel prevented him from doing so. According to a midrash, when Abraham and Isaac returned home, Sarah had died—perhaps from the shock of hearing that Isaac was being sacrificed. The story in Genesis of the near sacrifice of his son displays Abraham's willingness to obey God when he is tested. In Hebrew, the event is called the Akedah (עקדה), focusing visually on the "binding" of Isaac to the altar and calling forth an enormous amount of rabbinic interpretation through the ages. This story is always read in synagogue on the second day of Rosh Hashanah.

●meet *Rivka Imeynu* (Rebecca, Our Mother–רבקה אמנו)

Marrying someone from among our people has always been an important Jewish value, with exceptions of course, like Moses marrying Zipporah. Abraham sent his servant Eliezer from Canaan to find a wife for his and Sarah's son, Isaac, in Mesopotamia, the land of his birth. Eliezer brought camels, jewelry, and other gifts for the woman he hoped to find. To make sure he chose the finest wife for his master's son, he devised the following test. He would wait with his camels by the village well. When a girl came down to the well to fetch water for her family, he would ask her for a drink of water from her pitcher. The first girl to say, "Certainly I shall give you water, and I will water your animals as well" would merit the hand of Isaac in marriage. Can you understand the test?

When Rebecca came to the well to fetch water and Eliezer asked her for a drink, she offered some to him and also volunteered to give water to his camels. Eliezer knew then that she was the girl destined to be Isaac's wife, so he made Rebecca's father an offer of marriage on behalf of Isaac. It is significant that Rebecca herself agreed to leave her home and go to Canaan. Isaac brought Rebecca into his mother's tent, and they were married. Isaac loved her, and she was able to comfort him after the death of his mother, Sarah.

Like Sarah, Rebecca was infertile for a time; then she gave birth to twins. During her pregnancy, she could feel that something was wrong. When she asked God what was going on, God said, "Two nations are in your womb. One people shall be stronger than the other people, and the elder shall serve the younger" (Genesis 25:23).

When the twins were older, Jacob, the younger, persuaded Esau, the elder, to sell him his birthright as the firstborn in exchange for a bowl of lentil stew. Rebecca, who favored Jacob, then disguised him as Esau in order to receive his father's blessing. Isaac was old and blind by then, and was not sure whom he was blessing. He said, upon touching Jacob, "The voice is the voice of Jacob, but the hands are the hands of Esau" (Genesis 27:22). Isaac gave Jacob the blessing of the firstborn. When Esau learned what happened, he was very bitter. Isaac too was angry, for he favored Esau. Jacob paid for his deceit, by being deceived by others for the rest of his life.

◗ meet *Rachel Imeynu* (Rachel, Our Mother–רחל אמנו)

Jacob left home at his mother's urging because Rebecca feared for his life after he had tricked Esau. Jacob traveled to Rebecca's homeland, where her brother, Laban, still lived. There Jacob happened upon his cousin Rachel at the town well, and he instantly fell in love with her. Rachel had an older sister, Leah. It was the custom for the older sister to be married first, but when Jacob asked for Rachel's hand in marriage, Laban agreed, on one condition—that Jacob would work for seven years to become her husband. At the wedding, however, Laban switched the sisters (the bride wore a veil over her face)—just as Jacob had once been switched with his brother. Much to his surprise and dismay, Jacob found himself married to Leah. Nevertheless, he loved Rachel so much that he agreed to work for another seven years for her, and a week after he married Leah, he married Rachel. (Polygamy, or having more than one wife, was common at the time, and it was not unusual for a man's wives to be sisters.)

Leah immediately began bearing children, but Rachel did not. Rachel prayed to God and asked Jacob to pray for her, too. Years later, she gave birth to Joseph (who became Jacob's favorite son). And later still, she died giving birth to Benjamin, the youngest of the sons of Jacob. In the meantime, Rachel and Leah's maidservants, Bilhah and Zilpah, each had two sons by Jacob. (See Genesis 30.)

At the tomb of Rachel today, just outside Bethlehem, people come to receive blessings. Women, especially those experiencing infertility and problems in pregnancy, come to the tomb to pray.

◗ Meet *Leah Imeynu* (Leah, Our Mother–לאה אמנו)

Leah was an unappreciated wife. Even though she was able to bear more children than was Rachel, she was less loved by Jacob, and her children were not as cherished by their father. Leah is known for her eyes, which are described as *rakot* in Hebrew. That could mean "weak," "tender," or "delicate." A midrash says that her eyes became that way from crying. Leah suffered because of the cruel custom that the older child must marry before the younger and also because her marriage to Jacob was a deceit arranged by her father.

◗ Discuss

- How did Rebecca learn generosity?
- Rebecca, Isaac, and Jacob each had a favorite son. What do you think about parents having favorite children? Do you have a favorite parent?

- Was Rebecca's reason for changing the order of things a good one? What would you have done in her situation?
- What kinds of things do parents do to protect their children or promote their success? What do your parents do? What would you do if you were a parent?
- Do you believe younger children should wait to marry until their older siblings do? How much input—if any—should parents have in the choice of a child's spouse?

m'korot

Kadya Molodowsky (1894–1975) was a Polish poet who wrote in Yiddish. This poem, from a collection of her works translated by Kathryn Hellerstein, entitled *Paper Bridges,* refers to the four Mothers—Sarah, Rebecca, Rachel, and Leah—as guardians of certain kinds of earthly women.

For poor brides who were servant girls,
Mother Sarah draws forth from dim barrels
And pitchers sparkling wine.
Mother Sarah carries with both hands
A full pitcher to whom it is decreed.
And for streetwalkers
Dreaming of white wedding shoes,
Mother Sarah bears clear honey
In small saucers
To their tired mouths.
For high-born brides now poor,
Who blush to bring patched wash
Before their mother-in-law,
Mother Rebecca leads camels
Laden with white linen.
And when darkness spreads before their feet,
And all the camels kneel on the ground to rest,
Mother Rebecca measures linen ell by ell
From her fingers to her golden bracelet.

For those whose eyes are tired
From watching the neighborhood children,
And whose hands are thin from yearning
For a soft small body
And for the rocking of a cradle,
Mother Rachel brings healing leaves
Discovered on distant mountains,
And comforts them with a quiet word:
At any hour God may open the sealed womb.
For those who cry at night in lonely beds,
And have no one to share their sorrow,
Who talk to themselves with parched lips,
To them, Mother Leah comes quietly,
Her eyes covered with her pale hands.

Write

Write a piece of your own about Sarah, Rebecca, Rachel, and Leah. As you can see, each of the four Mothers has a distinct personality and each one speaks to a different life situation. To which Mother do you relate the most? Which one is most like your mother? Write a letter to one of the matriarchs—or your own mother—and tell her about an insight, question, or secret you have, something you think she could respond to with her own wisdom and compassion.

Fill in the gaps in a story as told in the Bible. Make up a story about one of the Mothers, something that you wonder about her.

Parents Today

Think about It

Before looking at Jewish sources on honoring parents, let's consider what *honor* means.

- Who in society is honored? Why? How do you honor someone?
- Consider the following people and whether or how they are honored: the queen of England when she makes a state visit to another country, the president of the United States, your favorite pop star, a firefighter who saves people in a house that is on fire.
- In Jewish tradition, it is said that your parents bring you into the physical world by giving you life, but your teachers bring you into the eternal world by teaching you Torah. Do you honor your teachers? Who else, besides your parents and grandparents, do you honor in your life? How can you show that you honor someone?
- When the Torah commands people to honor their parents, does it refer to loving them, or only to obligations, such as helping them with chores and being polite, or feeding and clothing them when they can't do this for themselves? Is honor equivalent to *respect*?
- What do your parents mean to you? How can you show them how you feel?
- What word would you use to describe the ideal relationship between a child and a parent?

m'korot

Look at these selections from Jewish sources and consider how they do or do not affect you today.

"Honor your father and your mother." —Exodus 20:12

"Honoring your parents is the most difficult mitzvah." —Jerusalem Talmud, *Peah* 1:1

"Blessed is He who has now freed me from the responsibility of this child."—*Genesis Rabbah* 63:10—a blessing said by parents at a child's bar/bat mitzvah, indicating the child is now old enough to be morally responsible.

"God accounts honor shown to parents as though it were shown to God, and, conversely, the neglect of honoring parents is regarded as an insult to God." —*Mechilta* on Exodus 20:12

To these positive commandments, Maimonides adds three negative ones: not to curse your father or mother, not to strike your father or mother, and not to rebel against the authority of your father or mother (*Sefer Hamitzvot,* Book 2, Nos. 318, 319, and 195). A separate but related mitzvah is to show deference to the elderly (Leviticus 19:32).

Write

Keep a journal for a week in which you record all your interactions with your parents, writing down what took place. How does the mitzvah of *kibud av va'em* enter into it? Discuss what happened with your parents. Come up with ways in which you could improve in honoring and respecting your parents.

Now make a list of things that you know upset your parents, then list ways you can rectify the situation. Following are three examples:

1   When I don't do my homework. *Make a conscious effort to do homework without being nagged.*

2   When I spend too much time on the phone or instant messaging. *Set time limits and plan activities.*

3   When I fight with my sibling(s). *Try to work out disagreements without raising my voice.*

Finally, list ten things your parents have done/do for you:

1   They brought me into this world (or adopted me).

2   _____

3   _____

4 _____

5 _____

6 _____

7 _____

8 _____

9 _____

10 _____

Ways I Can Honor My Parents

1 Take responsibility for my own Torah study.

2 Help with household tasks.

3 Show leadership in guiding my siblings' behavior.

4 Reach out to grandparents and an older generation and ask questions about their Jewish lives.

5 Write a letter or poem of appreciation.

6 Speak to them in an appreciative and respectful manner.

What else can you think of?

Getting to Know Your Parents

The better you know your parents, the easier it can be to honor and respect them. Here are questions to get you going on a fascinating interview with your parents. There are probably many events, people, and travels they have experienced about which you know nothing or very little. Your parents had a whole life before you came into it.

Set aside time to find out about this, if they are willing. Plan on one to two hours, and make sure you won't have any outside interruptions. Take notes or video your interview with them. Ask to see old photos and family movies. Ask them in which ways they honored *their* parents. How have times changed? However you decide to document the interview, make sure you keep it in a safe place. This interview will be a piece of family history that you might want to take out again and again. Eventually, you might want to show it to your children. You might even be starting a family tradition!

Interview Questions: You don't have to stick to these questions; they are just ideas to get you started. You might also want to use family photos and special keepsakes that are important to your parents to get them talking.

- Where were they born? If outside of North America, what was their immigration experience like? Why did their parents give birth to them there?
- Did they go to high school, college, graduate school? What did they major in?
- What are their occupations? What do their jobs entail?
- What are their hobbies and interests? What books do they read?
- Who are their friends? Who were their friends while they were growing up?
- What is unique about them?
- What do they like best about being a Jewish woman or man?
- What kind of Jewish education did they receive?
- Do they believe in God?
- What part of Judaism most appeals to them?
- Did they have a bat or bar mitzvah, and what was it like?
- What do they think is the reason to have a bat mitzvah?
- What do they want you to get out of your experience as a bat mitzvah?
- What historical events have they lived through, and what are their thoughts about them?

Do It FAMILY AND COMMUNITY *Mitzvot*

One good way to improve your relationship with your parents is to engage in fulfilling a mitzvah with them, such as the mitzvah of *limmud Torah* (Torah study–לימוד תורה) or of *tzedakah* (charity–צדקה). For *limmud Torah,* you might want to choose a text and study it together or make time during the week—perhaps Shabbat?—for family discussions of Jewish ideas.

Here are some suggestions for learning more about Judaism together with your parents:

- Spend part of each Shabbat learning Hebrew or reading *Ethics of the Fathers* together.
- Take a class together in which you learn more about Judaism.
- Form a Jewish book club with other parents and kids in which you read novels and stories by Jewish writers.

Tzedakah can be a way to work together for a cause that goes far beyond you and your parents. Here are some suggestions for family *tzedakah* projects:

- Volunteer at a soup kitchen.
- Sort through old clothes and give them to needy families.
- Set aside a *tzedakah* box for one cause and put coins in the box once a week (it is traditional to do this just before Shabbat begins).

Discuss

Think about the meaning of love and honor. Look them up in the dictionary if that would help. Discuss with your parents why we are commanded to honor our parents but are not commanded to love them.

When Honoring Parents Is a Problem

There are times when you cannot honor your parents. If you are being emotionally, physically, or sexually abused by a parent, how could you possibly honor him or her? Protecting your parents from being found out by your teachers, relatives, and friends because you feel you must honor them is not going to help anyone. No child deserves to be abused, and it is imperative to reach out for help.

If you are being abused and need help, there are some options for you to consider. Find an adult you can trust to talk about it with: a teacher, the parent of a friend, a rabbi, a counselor, or a doctor. Find a safe place for shelter if you need to leave your home. Call Jewish Family and Children's Services in your community.

Not as serious a problem, but something that can bother you: there may be times when your parent may curse or lie, or do something that you don't feel is ethical. This may not be directly abusive, but it can cause you discomfort or confusion. When possible, discuss the issue. It can be very useful to share observations and feelings.

Final Words

Someday you might be a parent. If that happens, how do you think you'll look back on this time in your life?

The struggles you are experiencing are important—and even valuable. Together with your parents, you are working on the task of growing up. This work takes into account their experiences as teens along with yours. Your parents brought you into the world and are raising you. If you were adopted or do not live with your birth parents, the adults who care for you brought you into their lives and are raising you. Up until now you have been their responsibility completely; that is changing. You are gaining responsibility and authority over your own life, but it doesn't happen in one day. You will work for many years to become a fulfilled, productive adult, a person who can make a living by honest work and give something back to the world. You and your parents are preparing for the time when you leave their care and go out into the world on your own. One day you will fly from their nest.

Learn לימוד:
Ma'akhil re'eyvim (feeding the hungry–מאכיל רעבים);
Hakhnasat orchim (inviting guests–הכנסת אורחים);
Kashrut (the laws of sanctifying food–כשרות)

Eating

*I like to eat—
and I think
about food a lot.*

Dear JGirl,

Will it be a burger and fries for lunch, a slice of pizza and a cola, or tuna on whole-grain bread and bottled water? Do you enjoy sitting in front of the TV with a bag of chips and a soft drink? Is your favorite snack a candy bar or grapes?

A new surge of hunger is typical for a girl your age, since your body is changing rapidly. You may also feel more tired, moodier, and grumpier than you used to feel. Believe it or not, all of these new-found feelings are strongly connected to nutrition. Because your bones are growing, you need more calcium. Because your energy level is changing, you need more protein and healthy carbohydrates. Because you are becoming a woman, your body requires many more minerals and vitamins than you needed as a child.

Besides feeling different physically, you may also change your attitudes toward food as you move into and through your teens.

Whereas once you could gobble down ten chocolate chip cookies and not feel stuffed, as you become older you may begin to have a different relationship with food.

In this chapter, you will find healthy ways to adjust to the new needs of your body. Today you are being bombarded with all sorts of negative messages about diet, weight, and body image. There is a positive way of looking at food, however: food is what keeps us alive and healthy. It protects us from disease and keeps us energized throughout the day. Food is not something to take for granted. You can feel your relationship with the earth as you eat, if you take the time to be aware of it. The focus of this chapter will be on developing a positive relationship with food and thus a positive relationship with your body.

Part of being Jewish means eating, talking, and celebrating—and sometimes not eating but rather, praying, and mourning. Most of our holidays contain some aspect of feasting or fasting. From potato latkes on Chanukah to matzah on Passover to cheese bourekas on Shavuot, food is a major part of Jewish celebration. Believe it or not, keeping kosher is a Jewish practice that can help you respect your food and your body.

B'teyavon! *(Enjoy your food! Dig in!–*בתיאבון*)*

Ali

Jewish Food

Learn

What does food mean to you? Food has different meanings at different times of the year, in different cultures, and in different families. Food relates to the following:

- Basic survival
- Nutrition
- Celebration of a particular holiday

- Hospitality and the nurturing qualities of the one who provides and prepares meals
- Preparation as an art form
- A means of passing down traditions and beliefs at meals and during their preparation
- Pleasure
- Denial
- What else?

The following list shows how particular foods are associated with each holiday in the Jewish year in a variety of Jewish cultures:

- Rosh Hashanah (New Year–ראש השנה)
  Apples and honey (sweetness for the coming year)
  Pomegranate (fertility, symbolized by many seeds)
  Fish head (the "head" of the year)
- Yom Kippur (Day of Atonement–יום כיפור)
  No food (so that we may "afflict" our bodies on this day of repentance and concentrate on other things)
- Sukkot (Harvest Festival; 40 Years in the Wilderness–סוכות)
  Wheat, barley, olives, pomegranates, grapes, figs, and dates (the seven species of the Land of Israel)
- Simchat Torah (Joy of Torah–שמחת תורה)
  Candy (sweetness of Torah)
- Chanukah (Festival of Lights; Maccabee victory over Syrian Greeks–חנוכה)
  Potato latkes, doughnuts (fried foods to commemorate the oil that lasted for eight days)
  Chocolate coins (Chanukah *gelt*)
- Tu B'Shvat (15th of Shvat, New Year for Trees–ט"ו בשבת)
  Fruits that come from trees, like carob, oranges, dates, and olives (Some fruits, such as strawberries, pineapples, grapes, and melons, don't fit into this category because they grow on bushes or vines.)

- Purim (Feast of Lots; Esther's Rescue of Persian Jews–פורים)

  A pastry called hamentaschen (Haman's ears), called *oznei Haman* in Israel

  Goodies for *mishloach manot* (gifts to send to other Jews)
- Pesach (Passover; Exodus from Egypt–פסח)

  Bone, chicken neck, or beet (commemorating lamb sacrifice)

  Egg (representing Jewish fertility and the cycle of life)

  Parsley or celery (green vegetable representing spring)

  Horseradish root (symbolizing the bitterness of slavery)

  Charoset (mixture of fruit, nuts, and wine symbolizing mortar for bricks)

  Matzo (the bread of affliction; no leavening was used because there was no time to let bread rise in the hasty flight from Egypt)
- Shavuot (Giving of the Torah on Mt. Sinai–שבועות)

  Cheese blintzes, cheesecake, and ice cream

  Any dairy food (because the words of Torah are "Milk and honey under your tongue."—Song of Songs 4:11)
- Tisha B'Av (9th of Av, Destruction of the Temple–תשעה באב)

  No food (to commemorate this and other Jewish tragedies)
- Shabbat (Weekly Day of Rest–שבת)

  Challah (recalls shewbread in the Temple)

  Matzah ball soup, gefilte fish (traditional Ashkenazi fare for Shabbat and Pesach)

  Cholent or *hamim* (a stew that simmers in a crockpot overnight)

⬤ m'korot The Forbidden Fruit

In the beginning there was the *adam,* a human being created from the dirt of the ground, *adamah.* In *Midrash Rabbah* the rabbis write that the *adam* was both male and female, joined back to back. The "creation of woman" was actually the separation of this being into distinct male and female parts. Eve, the woman, listened to the snake, who told her she would *not* die (as God had said) if she ate from the tree of knowledge of good and evil. The tree appealed to her eyes and to her intelligence (Genesis 3:6). So she ate its fruit and gave some to her husband also. Because this couple disobeyed the only command that God had given them—not to eat the fruit of just *one* tree, out of many trees—meant that they became mortal and were exiled from the Garden of Eden.

⬤ *m'korot* Manna from Heaven

While the Jews were in the wilderness for 40 years, God fed them by sending "manna" from heaven. Manna (מן) appeared on the ground and bushes every day like the morning dew. Manna was white and looked like coriander seed but is said to have tasted like whatever food each individual liked best. God instructed the Jewish People to gather the manna every day, and then on Friday to gather a double portion so they would not have to gather it on the Sabbath. This—and flocks of quail sent by God to pacify those who craved meat—sustained the Jews until they entered the Land of Israel.

⬤ Write

Here are some questions to think about. Use your journal to reflect on them and come up with your own questions as well:

- Imagine the fruit of the Tree of Knowledge. What did it look like, feel like, taste like, smell like? (Hint: Nowhere in the Bible is an "apple" mentioned.)
- What do you think made Eve trust the snake?
- What kind of a person was Eve? What sort of a friend do you think she would be? What did you think about her relationship with Adam?
- Why do you think God placed the forbidden fruit in the garden?

- What do you suppose was the Jews' reaction the first time they woke up and saw this strange white stuff everywhere?
- What would you have wanted the manna to taste like?

Meet Claudia Roden

Claudia, a Sephardi Jew, was born and raised in Cairo in the 1930s where she ate many kinds of food: Syrian, Iraqi, Italian, French, Turkish, and Egyptian. This background led her to become a cosmopolitan cook and connoisseur of different cuisines. Claudia has written cookbooks on Middle Eastern, Italian, and worldwide cuisines. *The Book of Jewish Food: An Odyssey from Samarkand to New York* is the story of her life, which she embedded in Jewish travel stories about different foods. That it is also a book of recipes is "icing on the cake." Here is an excerpt:

> The dishes of my aunt Latifa and her cook Nessim were the traditional ones of Jewish Syria. On Thursday night there was always lentil soup, rishta bi ats (homemade tagliatelle—pasta—with brown lentils), or rishta wa calsones (tagliatelle and ravioli stuffed with cheese) and fried fish. On Friday night there was chicken or veal sofrito with little fried potatoes cooked in the sauce under the chicken, kobeba—dumplings—and rice with pine nuts and pistachios. These and dozens more Syrian dishes are what we get when we visit our families in Los Angeles, Mexico, and Colombia, Paris and Geneva.

Think about It What Makes a Food Jewish?

What are your favorite Jewish foods? What are your favorite non-Jewish foods? What qualities make a food "Jewish"? Do you observe the mitzvah of *kashrut*, eating only kosher foods? Do you eat "partially kosher" or "kosher style"? Did you have different food favorites when you were younger? Have your tastes changed over time? What does food mean to you? What do you eat for breakfast, lunch, and dinner? Do you always eat three meals a day? Do you snack? Do you eat enough healthy food—whole grains and beans, other proteins (meat, dairy, soy, eggs, nuts), carbohydrates (rice, pasta, potatoes), vegetables, and fruits?

◗ Write

Judaism promotes a healthy attitude toward eating and food. Food is a symbol of health and freedom. The food served after Shabbat services, the *Oneg Shabbat*, is considered an expression of joy on the Sabbath. When there is a celebration such as a bat mitzvah or a wedding—or a *siyyum* (סיום) to celebrate completing a portion of Jewish learning—we eat food to celebrate. Some families have traditional Shabbat dinners on Friday nights, like weekly Thanksgiving dinners. Certain foods remind us of places, times, people, smells, and textures.

How do you feel about food? Do you like to prepare it, read recipes and food articles, cook it, eat it, or all of these?

What is one of your best food experiences? Do you remember the food your grandparents, other relatives, or friends cooked for you when you were younger?

◗ Do It Appreciating Food

It is traditional for Jews to pause and say a blessing (*bracha*–ברכה) both before and after eating. Another way to appreciate food is to slow down the process of eating. You should always try to make time to sit down and eat; eating on the run can cause digestive problems. Try the following:

Take a piece of fruit and bring it to the table. Now sit down. Before you start to eat it, take it in your hand and consider the fruit as if you had never seen it before. Maybe this is how Eve felt in the Garden of Eden!

Touch the fruit, feel its texture and its weight. Smell the fruit, inhale the aroma coming from it and think of where this fruit actually originated. Was it from a tree, a field, or a garden patch? Is the fruit local or imported? Imagine what the place it came from looks like.

Look at the fruit and notice its color, texture, shape, and pattern. Pause a moment to feel gratitude for this gift of nature. Now take a bite of the fruit and let it sit on your tongue for a moment as if you have never tasted anything like this before. Listen to the sound of it as you chew.

Continue to eat until you are done. Try to keep your attention on what you are eating, how it feels, smells, looks, sounds, and tastes. Try this with a whole meal sometime. It is a truly mind-altering experience which we could call "food meditation" or "food appreciation."

◗ Do It ⏐ Sharing Food

Ma'akhil re'evim (feeding the hungry) and *hakhnasat orchim* (inviting guests into one's home) are two more *mitzvot* that have to do with eating. Among Jews, it has always been a high priority to feed those who are hungry. In earlier times, when many more people were hungry, wedding celebrations were open to the entire community. That meant everybody. Serving everyone was not considered "charity"—the word *tzedakah* (צדקה) actually comes from "justice" (צדק)—and so hungry, poor, and disabled people did not have to feel degraded.

In ancient times, when traveling meant going great distances on foot through a searing desert, *hakhnasat orchim* was often a life-saving mitzvah. Abraham and Sarah were particularly devoted to this practice. In *parshat Lech Lecha* (Genesis 18), Abraham models this behavior by sitting at the entrance of his tent in the noonday heat and welcoming strangers. With great enthusiasm, he and Sarah hasten to provide water for washing and drinking and they prepare a great feast for their guests.

During the time of the Holy Temple in Jerusalem, when Jews were commanded to travel to Jerusalem for the three harvest festivals, *hakhnasat orchim* continued as a well-honored practice.

"No person ever remarked to another, "I couldn't find a bed to sleep in in Jerusalem"(Avot de-Rabbi Natan 33). Even today, many Jerusalemites go to the kotel (כותל-Western wall) close to sunset on Friday and invite total strangers to become their guests for Shabbat dinner. Shabbat hospitality continues as a mitzvah observed in Jewish communities worldwide.

"All who are hungry, let them come and eat!" We say these words every year at the Passover seder. See for yourself how to do this. Collect canned food or pasta from your house and from friends. Arrange to visit a food bank or a homeless shelter with an adult and some friends where you can drop off the food. Go online and find ways to donate time or money to programs that feed the hungry, both in your local community and in Israel.

Here are additional activities to fulfill the mitzvah of *ma'akhil re'eyvim:*

- Invite people living in your community who are not part of a family to a Shabbat meal or a regular meal. Family meals are a real treat for someone who always eats alone.
- Find out what local organizations work with the hungry and the homeless and ask if they need any help. Think about volunteering as part of your bat mitzvah activities.
- Donate used clothing to a homeless shelter or volunteer at a soup kitchen, either serving food or keeping company with the people who are eating.
- Instead of receiving gifts for your bat mitzvah, suggest a charity to which guests may donate in your honor.
- Bring the issue of malnourished people in the community to the attention of your local rabbi, the president of the congregation, the sisterhood of the synagogue, or the synagogue's social action committee. Ask if you can sit in at the annual board meeting to follow up on your ideas.
- Find out what restaurants and supermarkets do with their outdated or leftover food and see if you can arrange distributing it to a shelter or soup kitchen.

What Is *Kashrut*-כַּשְׁרוּת?

Learn

The Torah tells us repeatedly that the purpose of *mitzvot* is to sanctify our lives in imitation of the Divine. This idea is stated quite clearly in reference to the Jewish dietary laws known as *kashrut*. After listing the animals that are forbidden for Jews to eat, God says, "For I am *Adonai* (אֲדֹנָי) your God. You shall sanctify yourselves and be holy, for I am holy" (Leviticus 11:44). The adjective *kasher* means "proper and fit." Like many Yiddish and Hebrew words, *kasher* has entered the English language—as *kosher*—because there is no English word that quite conveys this meaning. Its usage extends beyond food to anything that is right and proper. For example, "My English teacher said it was kosher to leave early for my dentist appointment."

"Keeping kosher" with respect to food is a way of life that millions of Jews and Jewish communities observed in the past and continue to oberve. Your grandparents or great-grandparents probably have practiced kashrut, even if you do not today. Keeping kosher implies a way of looking at the world, a spiritual discipline, and a form of respect for food and eating. The purpose of laws around food is to foster our appreciation for food, to make us aware of what we are putting in our bodies, and to refine our relationship with the world around us. If you look closely at foods in your supermarket, you will notice that many of them carry a special symbol (Ⓤ or Ⓚ) showing their kosher certification.

After the flood, God gave Noah a set of laws that apply to all humanity—for example, to not murder, not to commit robbery, and to set up courts of law. These are called the Noahide Laws and consist of things that we today would regard as self-evident for the ethical functioning of a society. These laws included one dietary restriction: not to eat a limb torn off a live animal. (Evidently people did that!) The Hebrew word for "torn" is *treyf* and has come to mean all food that is not kosher.

For Jews, however, God instituted many more dietary restrictions. The laws of *kashrut* have helped to define the Jewish People since Biblical times. Keeping kosher means making distinctions and choices. "You are what you eat"—what you take into your body becomes part of you; therefore, take care about what you put there. Because the *mitzvot* are designed to make us sanctify life as much as possible, some Jews choose to take on as many of these practices as possible. Others, however, choose to take on just a few. As you learn more about being Jewish, you will decide which practices you wish to adopt. One may be keeping kosher. If you don't want to be a vegetarian, being kosher is an excellent way to sanctify meat eating.

The guidelines of *kashrut* fall into three categories: permitted versus forbidden animals, the prohibition of eating blood, and the separation of meat and milk.

Permitted versus forbidden animals. Animals that have split hooves and chew their cud are permitted; those that do not are forbidden. Thus cows, sheep, and goats are permitted; rabbits, pigs, and camels are not. Birds that eat grain and mostly walk on the ground are permitted—such as chickens, turkeys, and ducks. Birds of prey are forbidden. Fish must have fins and scales (e.g., salmon, flounder, carp, tuna). All shellfish is forbidden (e.g., shrimp, lobster, clams, oysters).

There doesn't seem to be a rational explanation for these laws. Traditional Jews believe there is intrinsic value in following *mitzvot* even when we don't know the reason for them. Early Reform Judaism decided that there were health reasons behind these laws that no longer are a source of concern and therefore could be abandoned. (Many Reform Jews are now taking a new look at *kashrut*.)

It turns out, interestingly, that the permitted mammals are herbivores and the forbidden ones are carnivores. Shellfish eat "garbage" from the bottom of the ocean. In ancient times it was considered unhealthy—spiritually as well as physically—to consume animals that kill and eat other animals, because the violent characteristics of such animals would enter the person who ate them (Mishnah, *Chullin* 3:6).

The prohibition of eating blood. Permitted mammals and birds must be slaughtered in a ritual way called *shechitah* (שכיטה), which involves a swift horizontal cut across the throat with an extremely sharp knife, so as to inflict the least possible pain on the animal. The blood is drained. We are not to eat blood, the Torah tells us, because the soul of an animal is in its blood (Leviticus 17:11). We may consume the flesh of an animal, but not its soul. This applies only to warm-blooded animals. Fish, which are cold-blooded, are not ritually slaughtered, nor is their blood drained.

The separation of meat and milk. The Torah tells us in three different places not to "boil a kid (i.e., a calf) in its mother's milk." A number of reasons are offered by the rabbis for this law, including a respect for the animal's sensibilities, but again it is a mitzvah for which there is no definite, obvious reason. The prohibition was extended from a goat kid to include *all* mammals and even birds (which are not milk-producing animals!). Food that is neither meat nor dairy is called *parve*. Vegetables, fruits, grains, fish, eggs, nuts, and oils may be eaten with either dairy or meat meals.

For thousands of years, every Jewish community practiced *kashrut* rigorously, adhering to the strictest observance of this law: using separate dishes, utensils, dishpans, sponges, and so forth for meat meals and dairy meals. Modern observance of *kashrut* is extremely varied. Some Jews continue the mitzvah rigorously, while others have completely abandoned it. Still others might choose to keep separate dishes at home but will eat vegetarian and dairy food outside the home, where the utensils are not kosher but the ingredients of the food are.

There are many more details to the laws of *kashrut*. But it is important to remember that these laws are more about our spiritual and psychological well-being than about our physical well-being. Restrictions on the foods we are allowed to consume help make us appreciative, grateful human beings. Some people say that eating according to kosher standards is a healthier way to live. In any case, one excellent purpose of *kashrut* is to refine our sensitivities and to make eating a conscious spiritual act.

As noted above, Jews observe different levels of *kashrut*. Some people do not keep kosher at all. Some keep kosher with respect to permitted and forbidden foods but not with respect to mixing meat and milk. Some people avoid serving meat and dairy together but use the same dishes for both types of meals, and some have separate sets of dishes for dairy and meat. Some keep kosher in their homes but not when they eat in restaurants; others choose to eat only in vegetarian or dairy restaurants. Whatever your decision or ideology about *kashrut*, as you mature you have the opportunity to decide whether *kashrut* is something you want to integrate into your life. If you want to keep kosher, but your parents don't, talk to a rabbi. She or he can help you to work out the difficulties in such a situation. It is important that families whose members adhere to different dietary rules learn to live and eat together.

Points for *Kashrut*

- Keeping kosher is a mitzvah in the Torah.
- Keeping kosher develops sensitivity toward animals, plants, and everything we eat.
- Keeping kosher strengthens Jewish identity and perpetuates an ancient and important tradition.
- Keeping kosher adds an element of holiness to the daily act of eating.
- Keeping kosher teaches discipline.
- Keeping kosher is a healthy way to eat (separating meat and cheese, for instance, limits the amount of animal fat you can have in one dish!).

Why I Started Keeping Kosher

"It wasn't about dishes, or law, or a way of life. It was only a way of feeling. Without any particular sense of obligation, I felt Jewish, I felt a valuable if occasional differentness, and I wanted to pass that on. I wanted my children to eat stuffed cabbage, then yearn for strudel, not ice cream or flan. It was the least way I could honor the grandmothers." —Elizabeth Ehrlich, *Miriam's Kitchen*

Why My Grandmother Stopped Keeping Kosher

"My mother grew up in a very religious home. The first time her mother broke the dietary laws was in the cattle-car on the way to Auschwitz. Someone had some ham, and people had to eat whatever food was available. People convinced her to have a little." —Karen Erdos

(Note: In a case where saving a life [pikuach nefesh–פיקוח נפש] *means violating a mitzvah, Jewish law states it is more important to save a life.)*

"Do not cook a young goat in its mother's milk." —Exodus 34:26

"You are to be a holy people to me. You shall not eat the meat of an animal in the field torn by a predator." —Exodus 22:30

"When you carefully observe the dietary laws, and eat slowly and deliberately, without hurriedly swallowing your food, your mind will be purified and the spirit of folly will be subdued." —Rabbi Nachman of Breslov, *Likutei Moharan* 1, 17:3

Blessings

Learn

Judaism makes time before and after a meal to praise God for the food one is eating. This elevates the physical experience of eating to a spiritual experience. By blessing the food before eating, you control your hunger and your body. Making a blessing gives you a chance to reflect on where the food comes from and to be grateful that it has been provided to you. By blessing first and digging in second, you are saying, "Before I respond to the growl in my stomach, I am going to pause and bless the Source of this food."

In traditional Judaism there are blessings to say before eating particular foods. For example, before eating a fruit from a tree, you give thanks to the Creator of "the fruit of the tree." Before eating a vegetable or a ground fruit, you say "the fruit of the earth." When eating bread with a meal, you wash your hands and then say a blessing called *hamotzi*. Bread has its own special blessing because it is seen as the most basic form of food, "the staff of life."

The blessing after the meal is known as *Birkat Hamazon* (Grace after Meals–ברכת המזון). It reminds us to be thankful for the food we have eaten; for God and the earth, the food's providers; for *Eretz Yisrael* (the Land of Israel–ארץ ישראל), and for peace in the world. It includes many lively songs. At Jewish day schools and summer camps, *Birkat Hamazon* is often transformed into a cheerlike prayer at the end of each meal. A shorter blessing is said if bread is not eaten.

Blessings may be said over food even if you don't keep kosher. However, you should not make a blessing over something blatantly nonkosher (e.g., pork, shellfish, non-kosher cuts of meat, meat and milk combinations). That wouldn't be kosher!

Do It

Here is a list of blessings for all the different types of foods:

- **Wine, grape juice**

  Barukh Atah Adonai, Eloheinu melekh ha'olam, borei pri hagafen.

  בּרוּך אתה ד', אלוֹהינוּ מלך העוֹלם, בּורא פרי הגפן.

  (Blessed are You, *Adonai,** our God, Ruler of the world, Who creates the fruit of the vine.)

  * *Adonai* is often used to stand in for the name of God, Y-H-V-H, which, according to Jewish teachings, may not be pronounced.

- **Handwashing (before any meal that includes bread)**

  Barukh Atah Adonai, Eloheinu melekh ha'olam, asher kid'shanu bemitzvotav vetzivanu al netilat yadayim.

  בּרוּך אתה ד',אלוֹהינוּ מלך העוֹלם, אשר קידשנוּ בּמצווֹתיו ,וּציבנוּ על נטילת ידיים.

  (Blessed are You, *Adonai,* our God, Ruler of the world, Who has sanctified us with the mitzvah of washing hands.)

- **Bread**

  Barukh Atah Adonai, Eloheinu melekh ha'olam, hamotzi lechem min ha'aretz.

  בּרוּך אתה ד', אלוֹהינוּ מלך העוֹלם, המוֹציא לחם מן הארץ.

  (Blessed are You, *Adonai,* our God, Ruler of the world, Who brings forth bread from the land.)

- **Cake, cookies, rice, pasta (all grain foods that are not bread)**

  Barukh Atah Adonai, Eloheinu melekh ha'olam, borei minei m'zonot.

  בּרוּך אתה ד', אלוֹהינוּ מלך העוֹלם, בּורא מיני מזונות.

  (Blessed are You, *Adonai,* our God, Ruler of the world, Who creates different kinds of food.)

- **Fruits and vegetables**

Barukh Atah Adonai, Eloheinu melekh ha'olam, borei pri ha'etz.

ברוך אתה ד', אלוהינו מלך העולם, בורא פרי האץ.

(Blessed are You, *Adonai,* our God, Ruler of the world, Who creates the fruit of the tree.)

Barukh Atah Adonai, Eloheinu melekh ha'olam, borei pri ha'adamah.

ברוך אתה ד', אלוהינו מלך העולם, בורא פרי האדמה.

(Blessed are You, *Adonai,* our God, Ruler of the world, Who creates the fruit of the earth.)

- **Anything else (including meat, dairy, fish, and eggs)**

Barukh Atah Adonai, Eloheinu melekh ha'olam, shehakol n'hiyeh bidvaro.

ברוך אתה ד',אלוהינו מלך העולם, שהכל נהיה בדברו.

(Blessed are You, *Adonai,* our God, Ruler of the world, through Whose word all things exist.)

Make a list of your 10 favorite foods. Go online to www.Chabad.org and see if you can find the right blessing for each one. Some people prefer to say a blessing that does not identify God with masculine words, such as the ones above. Hebrew itself can't be gender-neutral, because every noun is either masculine or feminine (as in many European languages). Marcia Falk, a contemporary Jewish poet, has written an entire prayerbook, *The Book of Blessings,* which offers alternative blessings that include feminine forms. Her version of the last blessing in the list above, for example, is *Nevarekh et Ein Hechayyim shehakol n'hiyeh bidvarah*–נברך את עין החיים שהכל נהיה בדברה (Let us bless the Source of Life through Whose word all things exist).

Eating Disorders *hafra'ot achilah*– הפרעות אכילה

Learn

Eating disorders often surface in adolescence. Chances are that you know someone who is suffering from anorexia or bulimia. How do you recognize an eating disorder? The following are some of the warning signs. A person with an eating disorder may:

- Gain or lose an excessive amount of weight during a short period of time.
- Exhibit significant changes in eating behavior (such as excessive dieting, eating alone behind closed doors, refusing to eat certain foods, or hurrying to the bathroom after meals in order to vomit or purge what she has eaten.
- Be preoccupied with food, weight, counting calories, and cooking for others.
- Have an irregular menstrual cycle.
- Have difficulty eating in public.
- Feel guilty about eating habits and ashamed or tormented by her body.
- Belligerently claim that she can eat the way she wants to.

An eating disorder is both an emotional and a medical problem and should be addressed. More information is available at the National Eating Disorders Association (www.nationaleatingdisorders.org), particularly the page "Eating Disorders and the Jewish Community," which explains the growing problem of eating disorders among Jews. If you or someone you know has an eating disorder or is displaying some of the symptoms of an eating disorder, then you are doing the mitzvah of *pikuach nefesh* (saving a life) by alerting an adult to the problem and making sure the person gets professional help.

There are three types of eating disorders: anorexia nervosa, bulimia nervosa, and compulsive overeating.

Anorexia nervosa. Anorexia essentially means starving your-self. People who do this have a distorted body image. They think they are overweight, begin to diet, and never stop. Exercise becomes an obsession, as do counting calories and avoiding real food. These victims dread having even an ounce of fat on their bodies. We know of a woman who eats and drinks nothing but tiny amounts of pita bread and diet cola. She looks like an inmate in a concentration camp. That may not be simply a coincidence—since she is the child of a survivor of the Holocaust and may be identifying with her parent. Anorexia can become a very aggressive disease, even causing death.

Bulimia nervosa. A person with this disorder eats by binging—for example, consuming a gallon of ice cream or an entire cake in one sitting—and then tries to take control by purg-ing—that is, inducing vomiting, consuming large amounts of laxatives, or over-exercising. The binging and purging cause dental, throat, and esophagus problems as well as injury to the kidneys and stomach. Sometimes bulimia is fatal.

Compulsive overeating. Like bulimia, this involves overeating and feeling out of control, but there is no purging. Instead, the overeater feels shame and disgust and may exhibit signs of depression, including mood changes and fatigue. She may even feel that her outer layer of fat protects her from the world.

Jewish girls may become vulnerable to eating disorders because of a clash between Jewish values and modern cultural values. First is the emphasis on food in Jewish life. There is a joke that goes, "Every Jewish holiday can be summed up in the following way: They tried to kill us, we survived—let's eat!" Second, there is a correlation between high pressure to succeed—often found in American Jewish families—and eating disorders. However, a person who looks very successful to the outside world may have a poor sense of self-worth inside. The tension between an outward appearance of accomplishment and an inner sense of failure can lead to an eating disorder. Third is that Jewish girls and women generally do not look like the typical image of white Anglo-Saxon "beauty": tall, thin, and blond. Ethnic women may develop an eating disorder as a result of trying to achieve this image. A little girl whose mother is constantly dieting may be particularly vulnerable to an eating disorder.

Pirkei Banot

"An eating disorder is not about food: it is about being empty on the inside. It is feeling that you have no right to exist. If you are anorexic, you are trying to make yourself disappear; if you are bulimic or a compulsive overeater, you are trying to fill the emptiness." —Rabbi Jennifer Rebecca Marx

"In the world of adolescent girls, thinness—sometimes at whatever cost—evokes profound jealousy. We lust for the perfect body. We crave control over our lives. Even when we publicly condemn those who 'control' their food intake, many of us privately admire their willpower." —Sarah Shandler, *Ophelia Speaks*

Final Words

Eating is not a simple act, even though we do it every day, several times a day, from the day we are born. Food is a gift that we are privileged to receive and eating is an expression of key elements in our culture, our families, and ourselves.

Jewish life makes use of food as a symbol at various points during the annual cycle and the life cycle. Food represents a plentiful harvest as well as our liberation from slavery. Food means celebration, whereas fasting denotes penitence and self-examination.

The *mitzvot* of *ma'akhil re'eyvim* and *hakhnasat orchim* demonstrate the Jewish belief that nobody should go hungry; nobody should be without food to eat or a place in which to sleep. Some Jews live on a diet that clearly distinguishes them from other people. Keeping kosher is a way of reminding you to think before you eat and not to take your food for granted. The practices of keeping kosher and making blessings remind us of the preciousness of food every time we eat and drink. They remind us that we are part of the Jewish people.

Eating disorders also make use of food and eating as symbols: control or loss of control, low self-esteem, and insecurity. If you or someone you know has an eating disorder, help is available.

Take eating seriously. Be conscious of what you eat, where on earth it came from, and how you are eating it. Eat to live, don't live to eat.

Mitzvah :מצוה

שמור את יום השבת לקדשו –(שמות 20:8)

Remember the Sabbath day to keep it holy. —Exodus 20:8

Resting

*I like to be active,
but all this stress is wearing me down!*

Dear JGirl,

When I was in high school, I sometimes took a "mental health day." I just needed to relax and chill out from the hectic pace and competition of school. People used to laugh when I would say how stressed out I was, but I remember feeling overwhelmed by the homework, the pressure to excel, and the extracurricular commitments I had made. The concept of Shabbat (the Sabbath) meant very little to me. Saturday was the day we sometimes went to synagogue in the morning and had a family lunch afterward, but the afternoon was always jam-packed.

Not until I came to live in Jerusalem in my early 20s did I see how over-programmed my life was. In Jerusalem, whether you are observant or not, the city really observes Shabbat. No buses run; most restaurants and stores are closed; people spend time with their families and friends. Because Shabbat transformed the very atmosphere of the city, I could not help but experience it on a new level. I realized I had never taken time to reflect on the week or to realize how grateful I was for the many blessings in my life. Shabbat provided me with the space and opportunity to do this.

The idea of taking one day a week to rest is an old one. Even God needed to rest after creating the world. The message Jews took from this? That we, too, need to stop. Our bodies need a break from sports practice, hanging out at the mall, and going to and from school, carrying our heavy backpacks. Our minds need a break from homework, listening to music, texting, and checking Facebook. On Shabbat it's time to shut off all the screens and make your own entertainment.

In Jewish tradition Shabbat begins 18 minutes before sundown on Friday and continues through Saturday 42 minutes after sundown—a full 25 hours. After turning off all their gadgets, people light candles, and focus on more spiritual activities. On Shabbat there's time to spend with family, good friends, or even just yourself. There's time to read for pleasure, sleep, enjoy delicious food, play with your baby cousins, and pray or meditate.

Rest is one of the most neglected and important activities for human beings, especially those who are still growing. A day of rest or even part of a day of rest can make up for all the exhaustion, emotional and physical, that you go through in a week. It helps you to think more clearly and be more productive when you return to school or work.

Shabbat Shalom! Have a great break!

Ali

Preparation for Shabbat

Shabbat is a Jewish way to quiet down and discover your connection to the universe and to something greater than yourself. It is a gift. Ahad Ha'am, a 19th-century Zionist thinker, said, "More than the Jewish people have kept Shabbat, Shabbat has kept the Jewish people." Shabbat is an experience that unites us, calms us, reminds us of what is important in our lives, and makes us distinctly Jewish. Shabbat makes us happy!

In his book *The Sabbath*, Abraham Joshua Heschel, a great 20th-century Jewish thinker, recommended that we set apart one day a week for freedom ... a day for being with ourselves, a day of detachment from the vulgar, of independence [from] external obligations, a day on which we stop worshipping the idols of technical civilization and a day on which we use no money.... Is there any institution that holds out a greater hope for [humanity's] progress than the Sabbath?

Shabbat is a day with guidelines for slowing down and taking time to just *be*. You may want to try following some or all of these guidelines to experience a day of rest in the Jewish tradition. You may just want to read about them and perhaps incorporate some of the suggestions that appeal to you in your daily life. If you've never observed Shabbat, start with one or two items and add more as you feel comfortable doing so. Or start with just one or two hours and see how you feel.

m'korot

"Remember the Sabbath day to keep it holy. Six days shall you labor and do all your work, but the seventh day is the Sabbath of *Adonai,* your God. You shall not do any work—you, your son or your daughter, your male or female servant, your cattle, or the stranger who is within your settlement. For in six days *Adonai* made the heaven and earth and sea and all that is in them, and rested on the seventh day. Therefore, *Adonai* blessed the seventh day and sanctified it." —Exodus 20:8–11

"What was created after it was already Shabbat? Tranquility, serenity, peace and quiet." —*Genesis Rabbah* 17:7

"'I have a precious gift in my treasure vault,' God told Moses. 'Its name is Shabbat. I intend to give this gift to the Jewish People. Go inform them.'" —Talmud, *Shabbat* 10b

"There was a monarch who prepared a special wedding canopy. It was intricately carved and adorned; the only thing missing was the bride. So too the world was created intricately and majestically, but the only thing missing was Shabbat." —*Genesis Rabbah* 10:9

"Shabbat adds a sweetness and a rhythm to the week, and all that is needed to begin observing this day of rest are two white candles, a glass of wine, two loaves of bread and a tasty meal with friends or family." —Bradley Shavit Artson, *It's a Mitzvah*

"A person should rise early on Friday morning in order to prepare all that is necessary for Shabbat. Even if one has a full staff in one's employ, one should make it one's business to prepare something personally in honor of the holy day. Thus Rabbi Chisda would mince the vegetables; Rabbah and Rabbi Yosef would chop wood; Rabbi Zeira would light the fire; Rabbi Nachman would arrange his house, bringing out those items needed for Shabbat and clearing away objects used only on the weekdays. We should all follow the examples of these sages and not say, 'Don't expect me to belittle myself with such menial activities!' On the contrary, it lends one dignity to honor Shabbat by preparing for its arrival." —*Shulchan Arukh, Orach Chaim* 250:1

Do It Ten Tips to Prepare for Shabbat

The fourth of the Ten Commandments that the Jewish People received on Mount Sinai was to observe the seventh day of the week (Saturday) as a day of rest, relaxation, and spiritual appreciation. Here are some suggestions for how you can prepare for the sweetness of Shabbat each week:

1 Light candles and say the blessing over them. Welcome Shabbat with singing.

2   Wear something special. On Shabbat it's customary to wear white.

3   Buy a treat (a chocolate bar or a magazine) and reserve it for Shabbat.

4   Help prepare a special meal. Treat the family to a special dessert!

5   Clean your room.

6   Invite a special friend over for Shabbat.

7   Call a grandparent or another relative or friend to wish him or her a good Shabbat.

8   Take a long bath or shower and polish your nails or do some yoga.

9   Talk about the portion of the week (the *parasha*– פרשה) at your Shabbat dinner.

10   Go to synagogue Saturday morning and hear the weekly Torah portion read and discussed.

11   Cozy up with a good book and experience the luxury and leisure of reading for pleasure.

12   Take a walk or a nap—or both!

Bringing Shabbat into Your Space

One way to add to a mitzvah is *hiddur mitzvah* (beautifying the mitzvah–חידור מצוה). This doesn't mean you have to spend lots of money, it just means spending more time and care on the mitzvah. For example, many people put flowers in their homes in honor of Shabbat. Some people make their own candles, candlesticks, challah covers, or kiddush cups or they use a special tablecloth or special dishes. This is beautifying the mitzvah of Shabbat.

Meet Queen Shabbat

In Jewish tradition, Shabbat is feminine. Maybe that sounds strange, but Shabbat has been personified as a female for centuries. Some other names of Shabbat are: Beloved of the Jewish People, Royal Queen, Mother, and Bride. Shabbat has been compared to all of these women in poetry, song, and prayer. The fact that men have been most of the writers of poetry, song, and prayer may account for the many images of Shabbat as feminine. In Hebrew all nouns are masculine or feminine. Shabbat is a feminine noun, as are *Torah, Jerusalem, Shekhinah* (God's Presence), and *Eretz Yisrael.* All of these—among the major features and concepts of Jewish life—are feminine.

Shabbat is the birthday of the world, celebrated weekly, and we feel like royalty by resting from worldly cares. Shabbat reminds us every week that we carry this royal spirit within us all the time, if we can just remember it. *Kol k'vodah bat melekh p'nimah* is a way of bringing the idea of the Sabbath Queen into everyday life.

Another way we bring to light the feminine nature of Shabbat is through a glorious song called *"Eishet Chayil"* (אישת חיל). This song is attributed to King Solomon and is found in the book of Proverbs (31:10). *"Eishet Chayil"* is a traditional song sung on Friday nights by a husband to his wife. In many homes, the children also sing it to their mother. In other homes, *"Eishet Chayil"* is sung to the Shabbat Queen or Bride, which has now "entered" the home. Regardless of a person's intention, *"Eishet Chayil"* is a beautiful poem expressing love, appreciation, and gratitude for the glory of women both in an earthly sense and in a mysterious, spiritual sense. Think of a special woman in your life whom you would like to praise and to whom you would like to show gratitude. Write about your feelings of appreciation for her in a poem or a card.

What does it mean to you that Shabbat and so many other Jewish ideas have a distinctly feminine character? Does this make you feel more connected to Shabbat in any way? How? Are there other female roles besides Queen and Bride that you see applying to Shabbat?

Shabbat haMalkah (the Sabbath Queen) and *Shabbat haKallah* (the Sabbath Bride) are two feminine aspects of the day of rest that frame Shabbat. *Shabbat haMalkah* represents structure and order, and *Shabbat haKallah* represents emotion and passion. Shabbat is described as a bride in *L'kha Dodi* (Come, My Beloved), a prayer composed by Rabbi Shlomo Halevy Alkabetz, who lived in the city of Safed in the 16th century.

L'kha dodi likrat kallah,	לך דודי לקראת כלה,
P'nei Shabbat n'kabelah.	פני שבת נקבלה.
Bo'i veshalom ateret ba'alah	בואי בשלום עטרת בעלה,
Gam besimchah, b'rinah uv'tzoholah	גם בשמחה, ברינה, ובצהלה,
Tokh emunei am segulah	תוך אמוני עם סגולה,
Bo'i kallah, bo'i kallah	בואי כלה, בואי כלה.

Come, my beloved, to welcome the bride,
The Shabbat presence, let us receive her.
Enter in peace, her husband's crown,
also in gladness, joy, and good cheer,
amid the faithful of a chosen people.
Enter, O Bride! Enter, O Bride!

● Learn Filling the World with Light

In Judaism, some *mitzvot* have deeper feminine connections. One traditional "women's mitzvah" is to set aside a piece of dough from the *challah* (Sabbath bread), as an imitation of what the priests in the Temple did. Anyone, male or female, who bakes bread for Shabbat should perform this mitzvah. (The piece of dough is usually thrown into the fire.)

Women also traditionally light the Sabbath candles. Some say this is because women are usually the "keepers of the flame" in the home; others say it is because of the feminine nature of Shabbat. In liberal Judaism, either women or men may light the candles, and in traditional Judaism a man lights them only if there is no woman in his home to do so.

After lighting the candles and reciting the blessing, we may add our own personal prayers for our families, our loved ones, and special needs. This helps us to focus on the meaning of bringing in Shabbat for the entire household. Here is an example: "As I light these candles, let the light come inside me and fill me and those around me with the presence of Shabbat."

Light a Candle and Relax

> At dusk, I kindled four candles
> And the Sabbath Queen came to me.
> Her countenance shone
> And the whole world became
> Sabbath …
> The song of the wind—
> Is the singing of Sabbath
> And the song of my heart
> Is the eternal Sabbath.
> —from "The Sabbath Song," by Kadya Molodowsky and
>   translated by Kathryn Hellerstein

This is the blessing over the candles that has been recited since at least the seventh century.

Barukh Atah Adonai, Eloheinu melekh ha'olam, asher kidshanu bemitzvotav, vetzivanu l'hadlik ner shel Shabbat.

ברוך אתה ד'ני, אלוהינו מלך העולם, אשר קדשנו
במצוותיו, וציונו להדליק נר של שבת.

(Blessed are You, *Adonai,* our God, Ruler of the world, Who has sanctified us with the *mitzvot* and commanded us to light the Sabbath candles.)

It is customary for an individual to light two candles because there are two commandments relating to Shabbat in the Torah: to remember it (Exodus 20:8) and to observe it (Deuteronomy 5:12). Some people light a candle for each member of the family. When the candles are lit, some people close their eyes, take a deep breath, and wave their hands over the candles in a circular motion, bringing the light inward. After they have said the blessing, they open their eyes, and Shabbat has arrived! Does your family have a special custom for lighting the Shabbat candles?

Write Reflections on Shabbat

Shabbat is a time for your body, mind, and soul to rest. In anticipation of this time, some people like to create something especially for Shabbat: bake a cake, write a poem or prayer, make something beautiful for the Shabbat table or your home. Write about Shabbat—about recharging yourself, connecting with people around meals, at synagogue services, and on walks. You could read what you write at the table or during an *Oneg Shabbat,* a Friday night celebration.

Imagine lighting the candles for Shabbat. Take a moment to write your own thoughts and prayers to be said at that time, in whatever language you like. Next time you light Shabbat candles, add your own prayers.

⬤ meet Malkah Shapiro

Malkah was a writer from a Polish family of Hasidic Jews before World War II. In her memoir, *The Rebbe's Daughter*, she describes a world that no longer exists because Nazis wiped it out during the Holocaust. Malkah was born in 1894 in Kozienice, Poland, to Rabbi Yerachmiel Moshe Hapstein and Brachah Tzipporah Gitl Twersky, both members of illustrious Hasidic families. In 1908 she married her cousin and went to live with his family near Warsaw. In 1926 she emigrated to the Land of Israel, where she published stories, poems, and essays in Hebrew-language journals. Her book *Mi'Din le'Rahamim: Sippurim me'Hatzrot ha'Admorim (From Severity to Mercy: Stories from the Courts of the Hasidic Rebbes)* was published in 1969.

Hasidism is a Jewish sect that arose in Eastern Europe in the 18th century as a reaction to the misery of the exile in Eastern Europe and the general desire for a more spiritual experience of Judaism. Led by the charismatic Rabbi Israel Ben Eliezer, known as the Baal Shem Tov, Hasidim (plural of Hasid) emphasized prayer through ecstatic dancing and singing and claimed that every Jew could connect with God through joy. There were different Hasidic groups, each one led by a charismatic rebbe (rabbi). They tried to live "in the Torah" at every moment.

In the following excerpt, Shapiro describes a special Shabbat in her home, which was the center of Hasidic life in the region. The Torah portion (*parasha*) for that Shabbat tells of the Crossing of the Red Sea. In it, the Children of Israel celebrate and sing the Song of the Sea (Exodus 15).

The women gathered for prayer in the dining room. When the cantor reading the Torah began chanting his sinuous trills for the Song at the Sea, the women rose from their benches and in a spirit of exaltation began chanting loudly with him. "Then Miriam the prophetess, Aaron's sister, took a timbrel in her hand, and all the women went out after her in dance with timbrels!" (Exodus 15:20). A cry of victory swept through the room.

◗ meet Shabbat Musicians

Listening to Jewish musicians who sing about Shabbat can be profoundly uplifting and, on Friday afternoon or before dark, a good way to prepare for the day of rest—whether you are cleaning, cooking, studying a Jewish text, or preparing to read Torah at services—is to listen to Jewish music. It will really put you in the mood!

Neshama Carlebach, daughter of the great Hasidic singing rabbi, Shlomo Carlebach, is the living legacy of a family that expressed its spirit and love of God through song, a crucial feature of Shabbat. Many of her songs are about faith in God and love for the land of Israel. Neshama has a very powerful voice. Some of her CDs are *Dancing with My Soul, Ani Shelach,* and *Journey.*

The late Debbie Friedman was one of the most widely known Jewish musicians in the world. With her lyrics and music, she encourages people to bring God into their everyday lives, to be spiritual every minute of the day rather than once a week at synagogue. She released over twenty different CDs, exploring everything from healing to overlooked women in the Bible to, of course, the celebration of Shabbat.

You may also enjoy listening to the Israeli singer Shuly Natan, and the Israeli-American singer, Noa, whose CD is called *Eye in the Sky.*

Experiencing Shabbat

Learn

An important Jewish concept is *na'aseh venishma*–נעשה ונשמע, which means "we will do and we will hear" (Exodus 24:8), meaning that first we will do what God wants, and then try to understand why later. At Sinai, God wanted to know if the Jewish People would accept the Ten Commandments. They were unsure of what the *mitzvot* meant and how to observe them, yet they were so profoundly moved by their relationship with God that they took a leap of faith and said, "Sure! We will do and obey these *mitzvot,* and eventually we will understand what they are all about."

The same is true for Shabbat. If you have never observed Shabbat before, it can seem like a daunting task to undertake for 25 hours. But if you allow yourself to experience it just once, together with other Jews, you'll understand much better what it is.

Shabbat has many rules that can seem overwhelming at first, so try just one and see how it feels. For example, instead of watching TV on Saturday afternoon, read a book, go for a walk, take a nap, or visit a friend or neighbor. See how you feel.

Genesis says that God created the world in six days, then rested on the seventh. With all that hard work, God realized that humanity would have a similar feeling after working, going to school, doing homework, and practicing basketball and a musical instrument all week. That is why God gifted the Jewish People with Shabbat.

The Torah says that Shabbat is a day when you should not do any work (Exodus 20:9–10). How does Jewish tradition define *work?* Many activities that are forbidden on the Sabbath don't seem like work (e.g., writing, listening to music, or talking on the phone). The principal activities involved in building the tabernacle, the temporary sanctuary in the desert, and later the Temple in Jerusalem, inspired the rabbis to specify 39 prohibitions for

Shabbat. These have been expanded for modern times. For example, the prohibition of kindling a fire now includes the use of electricity (although this is not strictly observed by all Jews). For modern people, letting go of our dependence on dishwashers, TVs, shopping, computers, and even cellphones and cars, reminds us that we are not masters of the world. If you've ever been caught in an electrical blackout because of a storm, you know how humbling it can be.

Refraining from work gives us the opportunity to enjoy and appreciate the many blessings in our lives. During the week we are so busy with school, homework, extracurricular activities, and our other daily activities that we barely have a moment to reflect on what we are grateful for. Also, by taking a break from the world of creation (which is what God did on the seventh day), we rejuvenate our creative selves. What work would you refrain from doing?

Below are some ways to celebrate Shabbat. The best way to start is to choose one to which you feel very drawn and practice it a few times, then go on to the next one that attracts you.

At the Shabbat Table

Learn

The Shabbat table represents the altar of the Temple (Ezekiel 41:22), and the *challah* represents the Temple shewbread, twelve loaves offered on that altar and then eaten by the Levites (Leviticus 24:5–9). We salt the *challah* as the priests salted sacrifices in the ancient Temple (Leviticus 2:13). After the destruction of the Temple, rabbinic Judaism endowed each Jewish home with attributes of the Temple through the celebration of Shabbat. Having dinner with family and friends is a chance to take time to eat, drink, talk, and sing for as long as you want. There is no rush at a Shabbat meal. There is usually a festive atmosphere to it, as people catch up after a hectic week, discuss opinions about the weekly Torah portion or current events, and generally enjoy each other's company.

FAQs about Shabbat

Here's a list of frequently asked questions about Shabbat that appeared in *Every Person's Guide to Shabbat* by Rabbi Ronald Isaacs.

Q: Why do we wave our hands over the candles before saying the blessing?

A: We should enjoy the candles and the light before we bless them.

Q: Why do we make Shabbat special by using kiddush wine?

A: Shabbat is like a bride, who deserves honor and wine, which is a sign of wealth, respect, and celebration.

Q: Why do we use two *challahs* at the meal?

A: When the Jews were in the desert, God sent them manna to eat. "And it came to pass that on the sixth day they gathered twice as much food" (Exodus 16:22). The two *challahs* represent the two portions of manna.

Q: Why do we sing "*Shalom Aleichem*" on Friday night?

A: According to the Talmud, when a person comes home from synagogue on Friday night, angels come along (Shabbat 119b). The song is to welcome these angels.

Q: Why do we wear fancy clothes on Shabbat?

A: Shabbat is different from all the other days of the week. In order to make it special, we dress in nice or new clothes. It is very common for Jews to wear white on Shabbat as an expression of the spiritual light inherent in the day.

Do It

One suggestion for your Shabbat table is for everyone to share a word of Torah or a positive story that happened to him or her during the week. This creates a cheerful atmosphere while giving everyone a chance to speak. You might want to read the weekly Torah portion ahead of time and offer your thoughts about it. Other people can ask questions about the story once the person is finished talking. These contributions can range from something personal to a world event. Not only do they enliven the conversation, they often lead to a lot of laughter!

Synagogue Services

Shabbat services may seem boring and long, especially when you don't understand Hebrew. Give them a second chance: Take a look around you and see what kinds of Shabbat services are available to you. If you have a friend who attends a synagogue, go with her. Or take another friend and go "*shul* hopping." See how Shabbat is observed at each synagogue.

Another option may be a service in someone's home led by a *havurah* (חבורה–a group of friends or like-minded people). The *havurah* movement originated in the 1960s as a result of several university students and professors getting together to lead prayers and Torah discussion themselves on Shabbat.

Synagogue may be overwhelming to people because they are not comfortable with the *siddur* (סידור), the prayerbook. One way to gain familiarity with it is to use a Hebrew-English *siddur* and focus on a single prayer. Listen to its sound as recited. Understand its meaning. Ask questions about the intentions of this prayer. Perhaps during the week you could do some further reading on this particular prayer. It will mean more to you as you continue to say it. Another great idea to increase your comfort level: Find out what resources there are in your community or online and learn Hebrew!

Pirkei Banot

Sylvia Boorstein is a meditation teacher, writer, and founder of the Spirit Rock Meditation Center in California. She has written many books on meditation, including *That's Funny, You Don't Look Buddhist: On Being a Faithful Jew and a Passionate Buddhist.* Born and raised in Brooklyn, New York, she grew up in an observant family and became interested in meditation in the late 1970s. Along with many other Jews, she found the spiritual techniques of Buddhism to be very useful in her own quest for God. The mother of four and grandmother of seven, she lives in California with her husband.

Illustrating that Shabbat and its celebrations can fit into our lives in many ways, here's what Boorstein has to say about her experience of the holy day.

I met my friend Eleanor when I was in the fifth grade and moved into a new school district. We went all the way through high school together. When we were in grade school, we spent Shabbat morning together at *shul* with our grandmothers. When we got bored with services, we walked around the block together and talked. I'm not sure what we talked about, but I guess we shared our secrets.

I like time for myself, just sitting and looking out a window, or lying in bed before I go to sleep or before I get up in the morning, to let the loose threads of my mind straighten themselves out. I wouldn't call it thinking, exactly. It's more like musing.

I notice these days that a fair amount of my *shul* time on Shabbat is that kind of musing. I know the liturgy well enough so that my eyes pass over the pages, my mouth says the words, and my body stands and sits at the appropriate times, but my mind often takes walks around the block. It comes back from time to time and notices the bar or bat mitzvah celebrant; learns who has gotten engaged or is about to be married, who is sick and needing prayers; what the interpretation of the Torah portion for that week is; and then it goes for a walk again. That's fine with me. It's a long morning, and I need the walks as much as I did when I was young.

The obvious difference between my walks long ago and my current walks is that now they happen while my body stays in *shul*. The other difference is how the secrets get told. These days, I tell them to myself.

◗ Do It | Shabbat Sleepovers

Plan a sleepover with one or more friends. You could have a special service for *Kabbalat Shabbat* (קבלת שבת–Receiving the Sabbath) at the home where the sleepover is going to be, then a meal together with singing. In the morning you could do some Torah study, perhaps examining the Torah portion of the week or something else of interest. You can arrange for a delicious lunch and perhaps a hike in the afternoon. Just a few suggestions for a really special experience!

Seudah Shlishit

At *Seudah Shlishit* (סעודה שלישית), the third meal, on Shabbat afternoon or early evening (depending on the time of year), the day is beginning to wane. The songs and tunes for this meal are more mellow than the songs for Friday night dinner. The prayers express a longing for Shabbat, which will be over soon. This is a good time to tell stories. The food at *Seudah Shlishit* is usually light: salads, vegetables, fruits, breads, and crackers. Taking the time to eat, sing, and share experiences in the late afternoon of Shabbat is a custom that developed from the idea that eating special food makes Shabbat a day of greater joy. Three meals in one day were a luxury in most Jewish societies in the past.

Havdalah

As we sanctify Shabbat from the other days of the week, our actions create a boundary between holy and mundane, or ordinary time. *Havdalah* (הבדלה) is the concluding celebration of that boundary and the ritual ushering in the new week. The ceremony includes a braided candle and aromatic spices and recitation of the blessing,

ברוך אתה ד' אלהינו מלך העולם, המבדיל בין קודש לחול, בין אור לחשך, בין ישראל לגוים, בין יום השביעי לששת ימי המעשה. ברוך אתה ד', המבדיל בין קודש לחול.

Barukh Atah Adonai Eloheinu melech ha'olam, hamavdil bein kodesh l'chol, bein or l'choshech, bein Yisrael la-goyim, bein yom hash'vi-i l'sheshet y'mei hama'aseh. Barukh Atah Adonai, hamavdil bein kodesh l'chol. (Note that the Hebrew word used in this blessing is "goyim." While you may hear the word "goy" used to mean non-Jew, the word actually means "nation" in Hebrew. "Goyim" refers to all nations other than Israel.)

(Praised are You, *Adonai* our God, Sovereign of the universe, Who distinguishes between sacred and secular, light and darkness, Israel and other peoples, the seventh day and the six days of labor. Praised are You, *Adonai*, who distinguishes between sacred and secular.)

Singing is a must, and the more people who are gathered together, the better. It can be done with or without musical instruments, depending on your level of observance. During *Havdalah* we light a candle of six braids symbolizing the other days of the week we are returning to, now that Shabbat is over. We make a blessing over sweet-smelling spices to represent the "extra soul" that Jewish tradition says we receive on Shabbat. The act of smelling the fragrant spices reminds us that Shabbat is also a "fragrance," which we'll smell again in a week. Finally, we make a blessing over a cup of wine, a ritual act we perform at both the beginning and the end of Shabbat.

⬤ Do It

This activity, created by Rebecca E. Kotkin, shows you how to make your own braided *Havdalah* candle.

All you need are a sheet of multicolored beeswax, wicks, and scissors, all available in a crafts store.

———

Cut the beeswax into strips approximately 8 inches by 2 inches. Cut the wicks into 8-inch pieces. You will need three strips of beeswax and three wicks for each candle.

Put a wick along the edge of the long side of a strip of beeswax so that half an inch of wick extends over the top of the wax. This will be the top of your candle. Fold the wax the long way over the wick so that the wick is "trapped" inside the strip of wax. Tightly roll the wax so that you have a long, thin candle.

Repeat with the remaining two strips of wax and wicks.

Put the bottoms of the three thin candles together and press the wax with your fingertips until it fuses together. (Beeswax becomes more malleable from the heat of your hand.) Carefully braid the candles, using light pressure on the wax to repair the cracks that come as you twist the candles together.

Enjoy using your candle to sanctify Shabbat and to carry a spark of Shabbat with you all week long.

One Step Further

We can also bring the tranquility of Shabbat into our weekday lives with the following activities:

- Meditating
- Being in nature
- Taking a bath
- Exercising
- Reading
- Breathing deeply
- Walking
- Learning Torah

Final Words

Whether you observe Shabbat in all its rituals and practices, or in some modified way that is still relaxing, you are partaking in the essence of Shabbat. The Torah says to remember and observe Shabbat. There are two aspects of Shabbat: One is the communal praying, eating, singing, and Torah study; the other is to refrain from everyday activities and concerns (e.g., jobs, money). People who observe Shabbat, in whatever manner, nurture themselves and allow themselves to feel their connection with God, the Jewish People, nature, and other human beings. They recognize their part in the larger universe. In fact, many people have learned from Judaism the importance of a day of rest for the health of humanity. To celebrate such a reminder every week is one of Judaism's greatest gifts.

Feeling Good 5 about My Body

I feel healthy most of the time, but sometimes I don't take good care of myself.

Dear JGirl,

You're coming into your own. Your body is changing in ways that mean you are now a woman. In some cultures in Africa, Asia, and the Middle East, for example, it's typical for girls your age to get married and start having babies. Some of your great-great-grandparents who lived in other countries were married not long after their bar mitzvah. You have other choices, however.

During your teen years you will become the person almost solely responsible for your health. Of course, your parents and other adults in your life will still make sure that you see a doctor when you need to and that you have food, clothes, and shelter, but it's up to you to learn to understand what your body is telling you and to keep it healthy.

The food you eat, how you exercise, what you do in your free time, how much sleep you get, whether or not you smoke or take drugs—all these are important for you to monitor, because ultimately you will become totally responsible for your own health and well-being. Someday you may decide that you want to become responsible for the health and well-being of others as well: your life partner, your children, your clients or patients or customers.

That's the key. Your health doesn't affect only you; it affects all the people around you, because they care about you and can be "infected" by you when you are sick—both by the germs you carry and by the low energy and depressed mood you project. The opposite is true, too. When you feel good in your body, soul, and mind, it's as if you are beaming out sunshine to the world. In this chapter you'll become familiar with some ideas that can help you to stay healthy and whole.

L'Chayyim! To life!
Penina

Your Health—Partners in Creation

Learn

Without your body, what are you? Your body is what allows you to be in the world, to go from one place to another, to get energy and nutrition from food in order to refuel, to perceive your environment around you, to experience every emotion, and to participate in your own life.

Modern Jews accept scientific ideas about creation, including the Big Bang and evolution, while they also believe that when God created the world, there was logic and order to the process. God created humans with the hope of having a sincere partnership. First God created land, plants and trees, and animals; then God immediately gave humans incredible responsibilities, opportunities, and privilege by giving the first mitzvah, "Be fruitful and multiply, fill the earth and be in charge of it" (Genesis 1:28). God encouraged us to take advantage of all that the world had to offer, yet in a structured, disciplined, and thoughtful way. God doesn't want us to be merely puppets in this world; we are instructed to be team players, active members striving to live in, partake of, enjoy, and improve this world. We therefore have a concept called *Shutafey l'ma'aseh bereishit* (שותפי למעשי בראשית), literally meaning "being partners in creation." We are in partnership with God regarding all creation—animals and plants, oceans and rivers, mountains and plains. A partnership is a cooperative effort. In this case, we are in a cooperative effort with God to keep creation going and to keep the world alive.

One of your main responsibilities now is to take good care of yourself: body, mind, and soul. Then as you grow and change, you will find your niche in the world. You will find a task that you are especially equipped to do and that will contribute to the world, its existence, and its betterment.

It is sometimes hard to remember that we are each a small part of one big whole. It is easy to feel separate from others as you go about your life each day, but in reality you are affected by everything that happens in this world: the weather, the economy, terrorism, war, and the good deeds of others.

m'korot

"Be very careful for your lives." —Deuteronomy 4:15

"To save one person is to save an entire world." —*Mishnah Sanhedrin* 4:37

"Blessed are you, *Adonai*, our God, Ruler of the world, Who has formed human beings with wisdom and created in them many passages and vessels. It is well known that if one of these were opened or one of these were closed, it would be impossible to exist." —Blessing after using the bathroom

"In the hour when *Adonai,* Blessed be God, created the first human, God took it and let it pass before all the trees in the Garden of Eden and said to it 'See my works, how fine and excellent they are! Now, all that I have created, for you have I created it. Think about this and do not corrupt and desolate My World, for if you corrupt it, there is no one to set it right after you.'" —*Lamentations Rabbah* 7:28

Write

In your journal or blog, consider the following questions:

- How do I treat myself?
- What kinds of things do I put into my body, my mind, my soul? (For example, I put lots of fruit into my body; I put lots of words from my reading into my mind; I take walks in nature to put air and sunshine into my soul.)
- How do I protect myself and take care of myself?
- How do I exercise?
- How do I rest?
- How do I feel about my body, my mind, my soul?

In the Image of God

Learn

We have seen that it is a mitzvah to treat ourselves with honor and respect, just as we would treat other people. Is there something special about our bodies, however? Is there a deeper reason for treating our bodies well than simply to stay healthy and alive? Yes, there is. We can learn this from the Book of Genesis, which repeats the phrases "God created" (ברא אלוהים–*bara Elohim*) and "in the image of God" (בצלם אלוהים–*betzelem Elohim*). When the Torah repeats a phrase or word, you can be sure something very important is being said. Remember, the Torah was first told orally. People didn't have written copies to read again and again. One of the best ways to make sure listeners remembered a key part of the story was to repeat it.

Jews typically do not get tattoos because of the belief that the body given us belongs to God and we should not mar or deface it. What does it mean to be created in the image of God? If God is not limited by having a physical incarnation, then how is it possible that we humans are created in God's image, since we, in fact, are very physical? How can the image of God be invisible?

One view of being created in the image of God is that the qualities of God are in each of us. God is said to be the third partner, with the parents, in the conception of a child. God's role in conception is to bestow the child with a soul, and through our souls we reflect God. (Unlike some religions, Judaism makes no claim as to *when* the soul enters the body.)

m'korot

> Thus God created human beings in God's own image; in
> the image of God, God created them; male and female
> God created them. —Genesis 1:27

Jewish tradition teaches that our bodies are vessels for our souls while we are alive, but that they ultimately belong to God. That is why a traditional Jew would never get a tattoo. What does this mean to you? What are you responsible for as custodian of your body?

Do It

Here are some things you can do to treat your body with honor and respect.

- Eat three nutritious meals a day. Avoid sugary and fatty snacks.
- Listen to your body; if you are tired, go to bed early. Take an afternoon nap if you need it.
- Do a variety of leisure activities—some energetic activities (such as karate or a brisk walk) and some restful activities (such as reading, hanging out with friends, or day-dreaming in a hammock).
- Try to do some kind of physical exercise three times a week. Make sure you have a proper warm-up and cool-down, and wear proper clothing and shoes. Even better, enroll in a yoga class or a fitness program. Try out for a sport at your school. Make plans to run or play tennis with a friend.
- Avoid alcohol, drugs, and cigarettes. These can damage your health, your school performance, and your relationships with your friends and family. Most of these substances are addictive and can cause severe physical and mental health problems that will get worse over time.
- Keep an eye on the number of hours you spend playing online games and social networking. Believe it or not, it wears you out. Give your body a break. Get up and stretch. Dance. Do yoga. Go out and get some fresh air.

Meet

Athletes are people who use all of the physical capabilities of their bodies to compete in sports—against other people, or sometimes even against themselves. Like all of us, athletes decide if they will treat their bodies with honor and respect. When they do train well and fairly, they often become role models for the rest of us.

Do you know about these Jewish female athletes?

- Margaret Bergmann-Lambert, German track and field athlete and high jump record setter, barred by the Nazis from the 1936 Summer Olympics for being Jewish
- Lillian Copeland, set six world records in three track and field events
- Julie Heldman, tennis, founder of Virginia Slims Tour
- Deena Kastor, fastest female marathoner in American history
- Helen Hines, three-time winner of New York Marathon and two-time winner of Boston Marathon, wheelchair divisions
- Dara Torres, swimming, twelve-time Olympic medalist
- Nicole Freedman, cycling, two-time U.S. National Champion
- Kerri Strug, gymnastics, Olympic Gold Medal winner
- Sasha Cohen, figure skating, Olympic medalist
- Sarah Hughes, figure skating, Olympic medalist
- Alexandra "Aly" Raisman, women's gymnastics, Olympic Gold Medal winner and team captain
- Sue Bird, basketball, Olympic Gold Medal winner and WNBA player
- Sade Jacobs, fencing, Olympic medalist
- And many more!

Pirkei Banot

"One thing I've learned from my body is it's OK to be different. You don't always have to fit in with the 'norm.' You can make your own norm." —Jodi, 13

"Sometimes this face looks so funny / That I hide it behind a book / Sometimes this face has so much class / That I have to sneak a second look." —Phoebe Snow, "Either or Both"

Do It

Sometimes it can be helpful to envision something in your mind in order to examine it more closely. Here is an exercise you can try yourself or try on a friend or in a group. To begin, sit in a comfortable way. Breathe in and out a few times to settle yourself down. Then imagine the following.

Someone has given you a small wrapped gift. Do not open it yet. What you have just been given is the most precious gift you will ever be given in your life. Now think about what is the most precious gift you have ever received. You will get only one of these in your whole lifetime. It is not tangible; it is not something to eat, and it is not the latest electronic gadget or a shopping spree at your favorite store. It is something that many people take for granted. How will you treat it if it's the most precious thing in your life? What will you do to ensure its well-being?

The "gift" is your health. It is yours to take care of forever.

Discuss

There are different kinds of health: spiritual, emotional, physical, and intellectual. How can you stay healthy in each of these areas? What are things that improve your health or hurt your health in each of these areas?

Write

Think about ways in which you would like to improve your health—mental, physical, emotional, and spiritual. Exercise, stress reduction, nutrition, yoga, prayer or meditation, and "down" time to relax or to write in your journal as a way of reflecting on your day are all ways for you to improve your health. What is the state of your health and your body now? Is it different now from what it was when you were younger? How? Take time to write about your reactions to this chapter and about the general state of your health. Just thinking about your health is a start in becoming healthier.

● Do It

The book *The 7 Habits of Highly Effective Teens* tackles the obstacles you will face as a teenager in a practical and understandable way. The following list is based on its suggested activity entitled "Baby Steps," a collection of ways you can make positive changes in your life.

Body

- Give up a bad habit, such as biting your nails, eating too much candy, or drinking too much soda, for one week, and see how you feel at the end of the week.
- Go to bed a half-hour earlier.
- Do something nice for your body (e.g., have a massage, go for a walk, or take a bath).

Mind

- Subscribe to a magazine that promotes healthy living or nutrition. Check out sites that send weekly Jewish voices to your inbox.
- Don't limit yourself to Facebook or news feeds. Go online and read part of a national newspaper every day; as a responsible adult, it is important for you to be well informed about current events in the world.
- Invite a friend to go to the museum instead of going to the mall.
- Give up Candy Crush or your favorite video "time–suck." (I know. It hurts!)

Soul

- Take a one-on-one outing with a family member to spend some quality time together: catch a ball game, see a movie, or go for ice cream.

- Begin to build a collection of something on Pinterest, You-Tube, or iTunes: favorite videos, selfies, movies, books, music, or great jokes; a hobby is a great way to relax.
- Learn to play a musical instrument or experiment with writing songs.

Drugs, Alcohol, and Jews: What's the Deal?

Some people are quick to dismiss the problem of drug and alchol abuse because they believe that "Jews don't have those problems." Although historically, Jews have had low rates of alcohol abuse compared to other groups, everything has changed in the 21st century. Jews in the United States are as susceptible to becoming addicted to drugs and alcohol as are people from any other group.

Your body is changing into the body of a woman. Although each girl's body has a different timetable for change, everyone will eventually mature. During this time you may feel insecure about your body. After all, it's not the body you have had ever since you can remember. It's not the body in all the pictures of you as a baby or little girl. Your core is undergoing so much change; you may wonder if you are the same person you were a year ago or a few months ago when you were still a "girl." You may wonder if you are normal. This, in turn, may influence you to use harmful substances to make you feel better about yourself.

Peer pressure is one of the most significant reasons you may be tempted to use drugs and alcohol. When you are going through this life-altering experience of becoming a woman, whom can you rely on to understand you except other girls going through the same thing? You tend to trust your friends even more than your parents and teachers. When friends tell you something is cool or okay, you are likely to believe them.

But this time in your life is also when you are ready to develop your own opinions about things and you are learning to listen to your own inner voice. This is a prime moment for you to remember the concept of *Kol k'vodah bat melekh p'nimah* (the true majesty of a royal daughter is inside her). This means that you have the right answers deep inside yourself on how you should react to the temptations or pressures to try drugs and alcohol. You have the most authentic, real answer inside yourself. Although you may be hearing lots of other voices that are encouraging you to smoke pot or drink vodka, before you make such choices, tap into your "royal voice" and listen carefully.

◗ Discuss

What is so appealing about alcohol and drugs, especially in the early years of adolescence? People use these substances for a variety of reasons:

- To feel grown up
- To fit in and belong
- To relax and feel good
- To take risks and rebel
- To satisfy curiosity

What do you think of these reasons? What could make *you* want to take drugs? What inner strength of yours would help you resist them? Does the fact that controlled substances are illegal for those under 21 affect your choices?

Drugs were not discussed much by the rabbis because their use did not become common until the 20th century. Drug and alcohol abuse affects people worldwide, and Jewish teens are no exception.

Cigarette smoking was not revealed to be an addiction or a health risk until a few decades ago. The Jewish community, like others, has only begun to come to grips with the health hazards of smoking. Many years ago, tobacco was actually used for medicinal purposes for people with digestive and eyesight problems. Recently, however, the Surgeon General's office has deemed smoking to be one of the leading causes of many cancers and other related diseases, and a number of rabbis have written official opinions saying that smoking goes against Jewish principles.

When used in moderation, alcohol is a significant part of Jewish ritual. Wine defines many important moments of the Jewish life cycle. It is always present for making *kiddush* (קידוש–the blessing over the wine) at joyous times: a circumcision, a bar or bat mitzvah, a wedding, or the four cups of wine required at Passover seders. It is also an essential part of the Jewish holidays. The use of wine each week on Shabbat may have spared Jews from drinking to excess, as it has always been part of the weekly routine in moderation. Even drinking to excess has been "legislated" in Judaism—to twice a year, on Purim and Simchat Torah.

DRUGS AND YOU

In recent times, as Jews have become part of secular culture, alcohol and drug abuse have become more of a problem in the Jewish community as well. Binge drinking, drug use, and addiction are a reality most young adults will deal with at some point. Ambulances are too often seen at high school and university events, transporting unconscious teens to emergency rooms. Some American cities have even sought federal aid for the high number of citizens—young and old—who become hooked on opiates and over-the-counter drugs. Don't despair. There are many things you can do to maintain your own health, even during a drug epidemic.

You may be curious about the feeling of being high or concerned that you don't want to be singled out as a goody-goody. So think ahead about how you might respond to social pressure when "everyone" seems to be partaking. Particularly if you are already taking medication for ADHD, anxiety, or another issue, you have to be extra careful with drugs and alcohol because of the danger of their interaction. Try to develop a good rapport with your doctor and verbalize your thoughts and concerns. Find a friend or an older sibling with whom you can confide your experiences.

- What are your thoughts on alcohol and recreational drug use? At what point do you think drug use becomes abuse?
- Do you have friends or acquaintances who take drugs? What do you think leads people to do that?
- How would you handle peer pressure when someone is trying to convince you to take drugs?

Final Words

We are all in this world and in this life together. We all come into this world naked, and we all go back to the earth when we die. What happens in between is up to us. We can let life slip through our hands, or we can live each moment as if it were the only one.

How will you live your life? Will you think often about how precious it is and savor those moments? Or will you hardly ever notice how you live and what you put into your body? Will you let yourself rest? Will you make the most of your body, stretching its limits of endurance and strength? Will you celebrate the abilities of your mind and work it, allow it to explore and wonder? How about your soul and spirit? Will you take time to develop the unseen parts of yourself?

Your health is up to you in so many ways. We are each born with a body, a mind, and a soul. Like farmers working the land, we must learn the tools to cultivate our health the best we can. In this way we also ensure the health of the earth, our home. All life on earth is connected. We have the chance to take the best things from the world, ingest the best foods, breathe the healthiest air, and behave in the healthiest manner. God continuously invites us to be an active partner in maintaining creation. This partnership not only follows Jewish precepts, it also leaves you feeling energized and vigorous. We have a great responsibility to care for our bodies just as we care for our homes, our forests, the animals around us, and the air we breathe. Becoming a JGirl means becoming partners with God, in whose image we are made, and being an active participant in living the healthiest possible physical, emotional, and spiritual life.

Liking Myself 6

*I want to fit in,
but I want to be
true to myself.*

Dear JGirl,

Who do you think is the most beautiful person in the world? There's no "right" answer to this question, of course. It all depends on what you think beauty is. As the old saying goes, "Beauty is in the eyes of the beholder." For some, beauty is a physical, external quality. For others, it is more intangible, an inner quality.

When do you feel beautiful? Is there someone you know and respect who radiates beauty? I'm not talking about wearing the "right" makeup and the "right" clothes. I'm talking about a person in whose presence you feel beautiful. Maybe it's your teacher, whose beauty appears when she teaches; your friend, whose beauty appears when she sings; your mother, whose beauty appears when she is comforting somebody; or your cousin, whose beauty appears when she plays basketball. True beauty is rarer than deep snow in Jerusalem; people flock to it the way birds flock to warmer climates—and it is lasting, not transient like youth.

The media—TV, movies, music, magazines, the Internet—all have an investment in making the definition of beauty dependent on your buying things. In this chapter there are many questions and tools to help you challenge popular notions of beauty. To protect yourself from being hypnotized by the "Buy this!" mantra pounding away at your brain whenever you watch or read or listen or go online, it can be helpful to learn critical tools that can keep you from being sucked into this. How can you possibly keep a true sense of yourself and the world when everyone is trying to sell you the newest, best, and most?

Girls and women are especially vulnerable to the belief that if we could only buy the product that would make us look a certain way, we would live happily ever after. That would be fine if life were a Disney movie or a fairy tale, where the shoe always fits Cinderella, Little Red Riding Hood escapes the Big Bad Wolf every time, and it only takes a kiss to wake up Sleeping Beauty after a hundred years. However, life is more complicated and intriguing than that. The search for beauty is a lifelong process.

Here's to your success!

Penina

Inner Beauty

Learn

At first Adam and Eve were both naked, "and they felt no shame" (Genesis 2:25). According to author Gila Manolson, they were able to see each other for who they were; that is, body and soul were one and the same, as in the way that small children view and ignore each other's nakedness. However, after Adam and Eve ate of the tree of the knowledge of good and evil, "the eyes of them both were opened, and they knew that they were naked" (Genesis 3:7). At this point, they lost the gift of insight and began to see body and soul as two separate parts of one person. Thus, the trait of seeing a person first as they appear on the outside began in the Garden of Eden.

It is so important to cultivate the inner qualities of listening to yourself and being true to yourself, which determine the way others think of you much more powerfully than your appearance does.

The mitzvah of *tzniut* is about "modesty"—in the sexual sense (how we dress and how we carry ourselves) as well as in the sense of humility (not being arrogant and vain and understanding the importance of respecting others). It is based on self-esteem. A lack of self-esteem often makes a person act arrogant or show off.

Remember how the evil queen in *Snow White* used to ask every day: "Mirror, mirror on the wall, who's the fairest of them all?" She had to keep checking because she was so unsure of herself, and she couldn't bear to hear that anyone else might be "fairer" than she was.

Self-esteem is more than how you feel about the way you look. It's how you feel about yourself deep inside where nobody else can see. It's unfortunate but true that today it is often difficult for girls to feel positive about their bodies and their appearances, and this affects how they feel about their inner selves.

TZNIUT–MODESTY

Tzniut defines a certain way of being in the world. *Kol k'vodah bat melekh p'nimah,* the phrase you have been seeing throughout this book, captures this way of being. At certain times in Jewish history, this verse has been interpreted to mean that women should stay inside the home. However, today it is understood in a different way. Among the Orthodox, *tzniut* refers both to a choice of clothing and to a modest personal style—no ego or arrogant behavior. *Tzniut* also applies to being well balanced and self-possessed, as in being confident in your innermost core and wanting to live from that core. That is the place of your authentic self, the place where you confront your true feelings and cannot hide from them.

It can be very difficult to reach this place when you feel pressure to assume an identity that may mask your real self. For example, the media constantly sends this message: If you want to be beautiful and cool, then you have to look the way we are telling you to look and be the way we are telling you to be in this ad, with this model, in this movie, on this television show. In recent years, "cool" has sometimes come to mean dressing in a sexually provocative way, but there is a belief in Judaism that says this detracts from women's dignity.

To remain true to yourself in spite of the constant pounding of these messages is a monumental task. The reward is that you will feel comfortable inside your own skin, and you will be able to convey this quality to others in your posture and your facial expression. Self-possession and grace will radiate from you. People will want to be around you and be like you, because they want to feel that deep inner peace as well.

One of the beauties of Judaism is that it applauds uniqueness in the world. The concept that encourages us to do this is called *Ner Hashem nishmat adam* (נר השם נשמת אדם–the lamp of God is the soul of a person). We believe that this special lamp is really a person's individuality. This means that latent within each person in the world is a special spark. Wonderfully, the world is filled with people each of whom is different from everyone else; all have their own individual insights, experiences, and dreams to share.

While being different might sometimes make you feel strange and scared, other times it probably makes you feel special and unique. Think about your DNA or your thumbprint. Its pattern is distinctive to you alone—no one else in the history of the world has ever had the same one. And like our individual thumbprints, each of us has some part of our inner soul that is unique to this world. Your job as you become a JGirl is to find your own uniqueness, and to let it shine.

meet Queen Vashti

We read the Book of Esther every Purim. Many JGirls know Queen Esther well and have probably been Queen Esther for a day early in their lives. In fact, the verse *kol k'vodah bat melekh p'nimah* could have been written for Esther. She worked quietly, secretly, and effectively to save the Jewish People. But how many of you have played Queen Vashti, a rebellious woman who was banished from the kingdom for saying "no" to the king? Interpreted from a modern perspective, the Vashti of the Megillah could be seen as retaining her modesty and responding with a sense of personal dignity.

m'korot

"Now it came to pass in the days of Ahashverosh.... He made a feast for all his princes and his servants. They gave them drinks in vessels of gold, and royal wine in abundance, according to the king's bounty. On the seventh day, when the king's heart was merry with wine, he commanded ... the seven chamberlains who served in the presence of King Ahashverosh to bring Queen Vashti before the king with the royal crown, to show the people and the princes her beauty, for she was fair to look upon. But Queen Vashti refused to come at the king's command by his chamberlains. Therefore, the king was very wrathful, and his anger burned in him."
—Esther 1:1–12

Write

Use your journal or blog to write down your reactions to this story. How do you relate to Vashti? Why didn't she obey the king's order? If you had been Vashti, how would you have handled it? Do you think Jews should celebrate Vashti at Purim? Do you think Vashti and Esther would have been friends?

● Meet Gabriela Brimmer (1947–2000)

Gabriela "Gaby" was a Mexican-Jewish woman born to two Holocaust survivors. Born with cerebral palsy, she was unable to speak or move her arms and legs. The only body parts with which she could communicate were her expressive face and her left big toe. She used to type out everything she wanted to say on a typewriter on the floor.

Gaby had a lifelong companion, Florencia Morales, who was her primary caregiver, interpreter, and mentor. With her help Gaby was able to attend a mainstream high school and the University of Mexico and eventually write her memoir, *Gaby: A True Story*, which was a sensation in Mexico and abroad. With Florencia she adopted a baby girl, whom they named Alma Florencia Brimmer. Gabriela Brimmer died in Mexico at the age of 53. Florencia and Alma still live in Mexico City together.

Gaby's memoir was adapted for Hollywood and made into a 1987 film (also called *Gaby: A True Story*) starring Liv Ullman and directed by Luis Mandoki. It is available as a book: *Gaby Brimmer: An Autobiography in Three Voices*, published by the Hadassah-Brandeis Institute.

The struggles Brimmer faced in being accepted by society as much more than "someone with cerebral palsy" demonstrate how difficult it is for people to see beyond the way a person looks. Yet, she not only succeeded, she became an activist on behalf of disabled people.

● Discuss You: The Target of Advertising

Television shows, advertisements, magazines, movies, videos, and websites bombard you every day with the same message: "Buy this, and you'll be happy! Look like this, and you'll be popular! Act like this, and you'll be successful!"

Of course they don't say this outright; they do research to figure out what is the best way to persuade you to buy their product. When is the last time you bought something or wanted to buy it because you saw your favorite singer on TV wearing it, using it, eating it, or driving it?

You need to be "media savvy" and know when you are being manipulated to buy something or to behave in a certain way. Is the typical *Cosmo Girl, Seventeen,* or *Elle Girl* model a normal female body type? In fact, supermodels are usually *not* healthy because they starve themselves to stay skinny. Most women do not reach 5'10" and weigh less than 120 pounds. All those pictures in the magazines beckoning you to "buy these clothes and you'll look just like them" are false advertising. Most of us will never look that way no matter what clothes we wear, what makeup we put on, what music we listen to, or what movies we see (and why should we want to? Beauty, remember, is in the eye of the beholder!).

One author holds that many girls divide themselves into "false" and "true" selves:

> With puberty, girls face enormous cultural pressure to split into false selves. The pressure comes from schools, magazines, music, television, advertisements and movies. It comes from peers. It comes from parents, from mothers who also suffered from the emphasis on being thin. Girls can be true to themselves and risk abandonment by their peers or they can reject their true selves and be socially acceptable. Most girls choose to be socially accepted and split into two selves, one that is authentic and one that is culturally scripted. In public they become who they are supposed to be. —Mary Pipher, *Reviving Ophelia*

Have you ever felt the urge to radically alter your own appearance—like getting a tattoo, a piercing, or a nose job? Do you feel any pressure to appear in a particular way at your bat mitzvah? What if you could see right through a person's clothes to their soul? How do you think it would change your impression of them? Remember Joseph and his coat of many colors? Look at the story in Genesis 37. How much did the way Joseph look affect his life? Was he the person everyone could see on the outside, or was he different inside?

Write

Write about your own struggle with "inner" and "outer" selves. Is there a quality that people do not see in you that you would like them to see?

Describe a quality of which only you are aware. Do you know other people with this quality? Is there a way in which you could make it easier for the people you care about to see this quality in you?

If you like, write a song, poem, or story about this quality.

Pirkei Banot

"Got new hat and shoes yesterday and I can see it would take but very little to make me give up my life to style, but I hope that such shall never be the case. I do not intend to give my life for 'a cap and bells' but I wish it were so easy for me to decide what I shall give my life up to." —Bella Weretnikow, 17, April 19, 1896

"Tues., 1 Aug. 1944. I'm awfully scared that everyone who knows me as I always am will discover that I have another side, a finer and better side. I'm afraid they'll laugh at me." —Anne Frank, in her last journal entry; she was 15 years old

"Flowers are very pretty, bodies of water are very pretty too. I think Ashanti is beautiful … I don't know her because she's famous and stuff, but she is really pretty. I think to be beautiful you have to show it in your actions, being honest, trustworthy, faithful, loving, understanding—all that I find beautiful." —Laura, 13

"Different people have different ways of being beautiful. Some people may have external beauty and others may have beauty in the way they think or act. It's up to each individual to create their own beauty." —Jesse, 15

Body Image

Judaism recognizes the pitfalls of low self-esteem. In the Bible, when the scouts were sent to the land of Israel, they came back and said, "We looked like grasshoppers to ourselves, and so we must have looked to them" (Numbers 13:33). If you think you are worthless and weak, others will also perceive you as such. It is very easy to fall into this "grasshopper mentality" during your teens because of the emotional, physical, and intellectual changes that are taking place within you.

You may not realize that you are falling prey to low self-esteem. Your outer appearance may feel awkward and uncomfortable. Your face may show your acne. Your hair might not "behave." You forget what it means to be valued for your uniqueness. Excellence comes to mean "most attractive."

Body image has a great deal to do with self-esteem. People with negative body image have a greater likelihood of developing eating disorders and are more likely to suffer from feelings of depression, isolation, low self-esteem, and obsession with weight loss. Let's look at the two sides of the body image coin.

With a negative body image, you are convinced that only other people are attractive and your body size or shape is a sign of personal failure; you feel ashamed, self-conscious, and anxious about your body; and you feel uncomfortable and awkward in your body.

With a positive body image, you have a clear, true perception of your shape—you see the various parts of your body as they really are; you celebrate and appreciate your natural body shape and you understand that a person's physical appearance says very little about their character and value as a person; and you feel comfortable and confident in your body. A beautiful body starts with a smile!

Write

Use the following questions to get you started as you write in your journal or blog.

- How do you see yourself when you look in the mirror or when you picture yourself in your mind?
- What do you believe about your own appearance? Include your memories, assumptions, and things others have told you about your appearance.
- How do you feel about your body, including your height, shape, and weight? What do you want to change about your body and why?
- Do you believe in cosmetic surgery?
- How do you sense and control your body as you move?

Do It

Try to remember 10 things you love about yourself, especially when you don't!

Girl power—What I love about myself:

1 _____

2 _____

3 _____

4 _____

5 _____

6 _____

7 _____

8 _____

9 _____

10 _____

Final Words

Inner and Outer Selves

Each of us has a side we show to the world and a side we keep to ourselves. Sometimes it takes a special person, a friend, a teacher or, perhaps, an older brother or sister to encourage us to show that hidden side to the world.

As Jews, we have often been labeled "different" by other people because of our beliefs and practices. You may feel this especially in December. People may wish you "Merry Christmas!" or "Happy Holidays!" even though you may have celebrated Chanukah weeks ago. The larger society wavers between accepting our differences and condemning them. Even in an environment where diversity seems to be respected, some people retain old anti-Semitic stereotypes. Because of this, some Jews have gone to great extremes to "fit in" with the people who are their neighbors. However, fitting in comes at a cost. You can lose yourself and your unique identity when you try to be just like everyone else.

As you become a bat mitzvah and after, you wrestle with how to integrate the various parts of you: girl and woman, Jew and plain human being, young child and mature adult. In the process of putting these parts together, you will probably feel doubts at times about who you really are. Are you the girl your parents and teachers say you are? Are you the girl your friends say you are? Are you the girl nobody really knows but you?

A fable told by Rabbi Nachman of Breslov (also spelled *Bratzlav*) describes a boy who could not fit in with the people around him, and people thought he was sick, so a Jew was brought in to "cure" him. Rabbi Nachman lived in eastern Europe from 1772 to 1810. He was the great-grandson of the Baal Shem Tov, the founder of Hasidism. Hasidism is a movement in Judaism that emphasizes dance, song, and prayer as forms of worship and ways to connect to the Creator. In Rabbi Nachman's day, these ideas appealed to many Jews who were not privileged to be Torah scholars, because it taught that there were other ways to reach God besides studying sacred texts. Storytelling was one of those ways. Rabbi Nachman was a master storyteller. Here is the story of the boy.

> Once upon a time there was a prince who thought he was a rooster. He wandered around the palace, clucking and crowing and waving his feathers just like a rooster. The king and queen were beside themselves. They needed a proper heir to the kingdom. How could their son ever become king?
>
> So a wise man was summoned. This man used to stay hidden in the woods, where he lived in a humble hut all by himself. But when he heard that the king and queen were desperately looking for someone to help their son, he immediately went to the palace.
>
> Right away, he was shown to the room where the prince stayed. He saw the prince sitting naked under a table, gobbling up crumbs. He asked to be left alone with the prince and sat down under the table with him and immediately took off his clothes. The prince looked at the man in wonder. Nobody had sat with him for such a long time.

The wise man began to talk about the fact that he, too, felt like a rooster. The prince and the man exchanged stories about being a rooster inside and outside the palace. Gradually, the prince began to trust the man.

One day, the wise man asked a servant to bring some hot soup and freshly baked bread from the palace kitchen. As soon as it came, the man began to eat. "Ah," he said, "this tastes so much better than crumbs! Why don't you try some?"

But the prince hesitated. Then the wise man said, "You know, you can eat this good human food and still be a rooster. Watch how I do it." The prince watched as the wise man ate and ate. His mouth began to water and he decided to try some hot soup. It was really good, and yet he still seemed to be a rooster.

So it went for several months. Gradually, the wise man convinced the prince to eat his food *at* the table instead of *under* it. Then he convinced the prince to put on clothes. Finally, the wise man invited the king and queen into the room to see their son's progress.

As soon as the royal couple saw the prince sitting at the table, eating real food, dressed in princely garb, they both kissed and hugged the wise man and their son. They were so happy to have him back. The wise man and the prince winked at each other. They knew they were still roosters underneath!

Becoming a Woman

*I am curious about sexuality,
but I am scared about it, too.*

Dear JGirl,

The way you feel about sex and sexuality is unique to you. You'll be interested in it when it's your time to be interested, when your hormones signal to you that your body is embarking on a new adventure. You may look at the rest of the human race in a more intense way, noticing details in people's bodies and in their ways of walking and talking that fascinate you. You may become aware of others looking at you in a more powerful way, too. You may size someone up and be attracted. Before you know it, you may feel ready to give yourself heart, soul, and body to this person to whom you feel drawn like a magnet. Your body seems as if it has a mind of its own, completely separate from your old, reasonable self.

How can this be? At the very beginning of your life, you were born into girlhood and all of its joys and hassles. Now you are being born into womanhood. You are being initiated into some of the great mysteries of life.

Unlike ancient times (for example, in the days of the Bible) when a woman's worth was almost totally dependent on her ability to bear sons, you live in a time when women are valued for many things, and you have years before you have to decide whether you want children.

You may begin to have sexual fantasies and desires now, even though you are not necessarily ready to act on them. It's all part of experiencing your new womanly body, your new role in the community as an adult perpetuating the human species. It's a big responsibility, and Judaism has wisdom to give you, especially about honoring the divine spark in yourself. It's also an exciting, pleasurable journey of self-discovery.

Happy and safe adventures!
Penina

YOUR BODY IS HOLY

Learn

In Jewish tradition the word *k'dushah* (קדושה–holiness) implies a separation—of what is sacred from what is everyday, of milk from meat, of the days of the week from Shabbat, for instance. Be mindful of what you are doing, rather than going from one thing to the next without giving it a thought. Acknowledge how amazing it is that you awaken each day, that each part of your body works the way it is supposed to. If you have health problems, think of how wonderful it is that you live in the advanced medical world of the twentieth century. Meanwhile, the sun rises again and you can start another day. As many Jews say, when acknowledging the wonders of life, *Barukh HaShem!* (ברוך השם!–God bless.)

Jewish tradition provides ways for us to think about what we are going to do and notice how we are feeling. It helps us take time to appreciate the life force that courses through us, the same life force that courses through the universe. This is *k'dushah,* and the mitzvah connected with this value is *K'doshim tihyu* (קדושים תהיו–you shall be holy).

"You shall be holy because I am holy," God says to the Jewish People in Leviticus 19:2. Holiness is an inner quality that each person has, a quality that allows us to connect with something greater than us and greater than our lives here on earth. It is like the awe that we feel upon seeing a rainbow, the ocean, or the earth from an airplane, for example. *K'doshim tihyu* means that you inhabit a sacred space and your body is a sacred space, a holy temple.

Considering the story of Adam and Eve in the Garden of Eden offers an opportunity to explore feelings and attitudes about sex and sexuality in a Jewish context. Do you remember that God did not want Adam and Eve to have the knowledge they could get by doing as the snake suggested and eating from the tree? God said to Adam and Eve, "Of every tree in the garden you may freely eat; but of the tree of the knowledge of good and evil, you shall not eat of it; for on the day that you eat of it, you will surely die" (Genesis 2:16–17).

WHAT WAS GOD WORRIED ABOUT?

What was God worried about? Why was this knowledge so dangerous? Could the "dying" that would come about by eating from the tree be something other than a physical death? Could it be, instead, a fundamental change in Adam and Eve that would make them essentially different beings?

Knowledge can do that. A new world opened up to you when you started to talk. People responded to you in a different way. They could know what you wanted or didn't want, rather than having to guess what your needs were. When you began to read, you could learn about things that were not right in front of you. You gained a key to knowing about all sorts of things—some exciting, some boring, some interesting, some dangerous, some beautiful, and some repulsive.

When Adam and Eve ate the forbidden fruit of knowledge, they began to understand that they were two separate beings who could come together and draw apart. They also understood that they were physically different. "The eyes of both of them were opened, and they knew that they were naked; they sewed fig leaves together and made themselves loincloths" (Genesis 3:7).

When Adam and Eve left the Garden of Eden, where their every need had been provided for, the man had to work hard to make food come out of the ground, and the woman had to work hard to make new life come out of her body. Adam and Eve's independence came at a cost. Your independence will also have negative and positive aspects. Now is a time in your life where your body is changing along with your attitudes and desires. You will never be the same again. You have left the small "garden" of childhood for the larger world of adulthood. Now you'll spend the better part of your life learning the unique ways in which you can give to the world.

SEX AND SPIRITUALITY

Sex preserves every living species, but in Jewish tradition sex also has a greater spiritual meaning. It is one of the things that sustains a marriage and brings two people closer together. The sex drive parallels the spiritual drive that can connect people to a force that is larger than themselves. The Jewish view of sexuality transforms this ordinary act into a sacred one.

In Judaism, sex is supposed to happen within a committed, loving relationship, preferably marriage. Orthodox Judaism limits this to mature adults of the opposite sex. Reform, Reconstructionist, and Conservative Judaism accept same-sex relationships that meet the same criteria of maturity, love, and commitment.

Your way of thinking about sex has a great deal to do with self-esteem. If you feel positive about yourself, you will have an easier time making decisions about your sexual activity as you mature. Your level of comfort with your body will also determine how you feel about your sexuality.

Teenage girls are often pressured to have sex before they are ready—by boys and, now, even by society (through mass media). It is very difficult, sometimes, to be able to separate your own thoughts from your physical feelings, and your own desires from the overly sexualized culture we live in. Self-esteem and belief in the strength of your own convictions can help you to resist such pressure and wait for emotional and physical maturity before becoming sexually active.

◖Write

Sit down at your computer and write any thoughts that have occurred to you so far in reading this chapter. What messages has society already given you about sex? How might Jewish attitudes toward sex and spirituality influence how you think of your own sexuality? Do you respect or even admire sexually active teens? Why or why not?

◖Meet Dr. Ruth Westheimer

Dr. Ruth is a psychosexual therapist born in Frankfurt, Germany, in 1928, whose parents were murdered in Auschwitz. In 1942 at age 16, she moved to Palestine and fought for Israel's independence as a member of the Haganah (the underground Jewish fighting force that was the precursor of the Israeli Army).

Now a resident of New York City, Dr. Ruth advocates sexual intimacy as an important part of human life and asserts that it should take place within the bounds of a loving and committed relationship. She is a columnist, a media personality, and an author. She has even hosted a show just for teens, called "What's Up, Dr. Ruth?"

Dr. Ruth remains a devoted Zionist, visiting Israel frequently and contributing to charity there. She has helped many people talk openly about their sexuality and all the questions they have about sex.

Meet Judy Blume

Judy is an author of books for children and young adults who dared to tackle some of the most difficult issues facing teens, among them, sexuality.

Born in New Jersey in 1938, Judy graduated from New York University. She began writing for children as a suburban mom, searching for a way to express herself. Judy Blume sold her first story, "The One in the Middle Is a Green Kangaroo," to a magazine in 1969. She has since written many books for children, teenagers, and adults, selling more than 75 million copies. Her work has been translated into more than 20 languages. Judy established the KIDS Fund in 1981 to foster better communication between parents and children, and won the American Library Association's Margaret A. Edwards Award for Lifetime Achievement in 1996.

Judy is often praised for her ability to relate to young people and discuss sensitive subjects openly. Do you know her books?

Think about It

The successes of Dr. Ruth and Judy Blume come from their knowledge and for understanding ways of conveying it. Do you know someone you can talk to and ask questions about sex, someone who will give you accurate information? It could be your mother, your big sister, another older relative, a friend you trust, your doctor, or your bat mitzvah teacher. It's important to have a female friend who has more life experience than you do, one to whom you feel comfortable talking about sex and the changes going on in your body.

Celebrating Your Period

Jewish girls around the world have had a variety of coming-of-age rituals marking their first monthly period. In some cultures, the coming-of-age ritual was a wedding! The practice among Jews in Ethiopia used to be to make an arranged marriage for a girl before puberty. The girl would live in her in-laws' house as part of the family, but she and her husband would not share a bed until she began to menstruate. In eastern Europe in the 18th and 19th centuries, boys and girls age 12 and older would get married and live as a couple in one of their parents' homes.

Bat mitzvah is a recognition by the Jewish community that a girl has come of age physically and is therefore ready to be an adult member of that community, spiritually and according to Jewish law. There is no link between the bat mitzvah ceremony and menarche (the onset of menstruation), however. Bat mitzvah celebrations occur at age 12 or 13 regardless of when a girl begins to menstruate. That is why it is so important to take time during preparations for your bat mitzvah to focus on the connection between the physical changes taking place in the body and what they mean for you as a Jewish woman.

THE INNER YOU

At the same time, remember that physical changes are an outer sign that certain qualities are growing within you as well—*Kol k'vodah bat melekh p'nimah* (the true majesty of a royal daughter is inside her). You may be changing in your own eyes and in the eyes of the world, but the inner changes are much deeper and represent an even greater shift in your being. When you reach the age of bat mitzvah, your community sees in you the potential for carrying on Jewish tradition and for keeping it alive by bringing it into yourself.

This is similar to the lighting of Shabbat candles, which has more than one layer of meaning. When you light the candles, you bring their light into your home by forming circles with your hands. This is an outer sign that Shabbat has begun. At the same time, you bring the light of Shabbat into yourself—that is, you invite the inspiration and comfort of *Shabbat haMalkah* into your inner world as your female ancestors have done for centuries.

THE BLOOD TABOO

Ancient peoples both dreaded and honored blood because, as it says in Leviticus (17:11), "the life of the flesh is in the blood." *Kashrut* demands that we not consume rare meat because of this. Traditional Judaism also has a strong taboo against male contact with menstrual blood. Many people have mistaken this taboo for a negative opinion about the blood and the female body, but as we noted earlier, such "separation" is a sign of holiness in Judaism. Menstruation is a miracle that signals your capacity to bring life into being. Traditional Judaism uses menstruation as a reason for a woman to have a time for herself, to be with her body alone.

In some cultures a girl's first menstruation is cause for celebration. Shortly after a Navajo girl has her first period, she participates in a ceremony during which, according to Navajo belief, she becomes a mythical character called Changing Woman, daughter of Mother Earth and Father Sky. Changing Woman is responsible for the fertility of the earth and human beings. She becomes the girl's guardian spirit, teaching and advising her from that time on, and the community of women who have witnessed the ceremony provide support, both spiritual and material, to the girl.

Some Jews are creating new rituals and new blessings to emphasize the positive, life-giving associations of menstruation. Goldie Milgram, an author and spiritual leader in New York City, has composed the following ritual.

Welcome to the sisterhood, may your life as a woman be filled with blessing! When your flow ceases, [here's] a little ritual that you can do every month to honor the return of your body cycle, to ensure your well-being, and to welcome the restoration of your energy. [When you're ready,] put a pan out to collect rainwater to add to your bath. Just as you are made of *mayim hayim*, living waters, so it is our custom to immerse in a *mikvah*, a pool of living waters at the end of a cycle of life, which is the egg that has finished its season in your body.

Put in perfumed bubbles or soothing salts, if you'd like. As you rest in the tub, you can review the month gone by. What is it that has lost potential this month, what are you letting go of? What is developing in fascinating ways that you wish to nurture? What blessings and strengths do you hope to draw upon, as a new cycle of days begins? Later, you might write these thoughts in a diary. You can shape your thoughts into a prayer and whisper them—that is a tradition that goes all the way back to Hannah in the Bible.

Your monthly *mikvah* is also an important time to check over your body, which is developing so beautifully every day. It is good to enjoy and marvel at the woman you are becoming. [You may want to write the following *mikvah* blessing on a hand towel using washable fabric paint.] Recite [the *mikvah* blessing] and perhaps experience the tradition of the bath as a womb; slip under the water and emerge reborn, into a new month of living and new season of your life. This month, this *mikvah*, is a celebration of your physical arrival as a woman. Mazel tov!

The blessing for immersion is simple:

B'rukhah at Ya, ha-Sh'khinah, chei ha-olamim, asher kidashtanu b'mitzvotekha v'tzivtanu al ha-t'vilah.

ברוך אתה די, השכינה, חי עולמים, אשר קדשנו במצוותיה, וציונו על התבילה

Blessed are you *Shekhinah* [the feminine aspect of God], life of all the worlds, who has made us holy with your mitzvot, and commanded us on immersion.

[Here is another blessing that you may want to recite during this ritual.]

B'shem El Shaddai ekra Melekh ha-olam avakesh b'riut u-sh'leimut b'gufi u-v'ruchi b'chayei avarekh et Adonai Rofei kol basar, u-Mafli la'asot.

בשם אל שדי אקרא, מלך העולם, אבקש בריאות ושלימות בגופי ורוחי בחיי אברך את ד', רופא כל בשר, ומפליא לעשות

In the name of El Shaddai [Nurturing One], I call out Sovereign of Eternity, I request health and wholeness in my body and spirit. With my life I will bless God (My Threshold), Healer of all flesh, Maker of miracles.

Rabbi Elyse Goldstein has adapted the traditional blessing said by men every morning in the synagogue, "Blessed are You, Lord our God, Ruler of the World, who has not made me a woman." While rabbis explain the blessing as gratitude for men being assigned more *mitzvot* than women, this blessing has become offensive to many Jewish women in recent times. Rabbi Goldstein's revised version allows us to affirm our creation as women at the moment we get our period once again:

Barukh Atah Adonai, Eloheinu melekh ha'olam, she'asani ishah.

ברוך אתה ד', מלך העולם, שעשני אשה.

Blessed are You, *Adonai* our God, Ruler of the world, Who has made me a woman.

Pirkei Banot

"When I was a freshman in college, [I started] wondering why I had always thought of my period as a bad thing. It was an unequivocal sign of my femaleness. So, why wasn't it just a sign of my normalcy? Why was I still trying to covertly detach a pad from my underwear silently enough so that the person in the next stall—another woman with her own period—wouldn't hear? Why did I both dread and impatiently await it?...

"I decided to try to consciously think of my period as a tolerable, maybe even neat, part of my life. For the first few cycles it was a struggle. Whenever I felt a cramp, in particular, it was not so easy to just say, 'Oh, la di da, my body is beautiful. I can feel it working its magic!' But soon the cramps nearly ceased altogether. And when they [do] come on, as immediately as I [can], I [do] something to make myself feel better. Sometimes it is chocolate. Sometimes it is crumpling up into a ball on my bed or some other quiet place. And in my best moments, I will get into a really comfortable yogic relaxation pose....

"I started to see my sour mood in the week approaching my period as a kind of homesickness. I felt waves of relief when it finally came. My period thus became my coming home, my time when I feel the most myself and the most in tune with the world; a space where there is clarity and light and reason to celebrate how ... amazing my body is.... [It is] a reminder of the mysteries that lie under my skin, physical and mystical." —Michelle

Blessed Be God Who Made Me a Woman

Blessed be God, who made me a woman,
Who made me Eve, mother of all the living;
And who made me Sarah, the ruler of her home;
And who made me Rebecca, the educator;
And who made me Rachel, the beloved one;
And who made me Leah, the fruitful one.

Blessed be God, who made me a woman,
Who made me Tamar, the avenger;
And who made me Shifrah and who made me Puah,
    the rebels;
And who made me Yocheved, the mother;

And who made me Miriam, the sister;
And who made me Tzipporah, the wife.

Blessed be God, who made me a woman,
Who made me Devorah, the judge;
And who made me Yael, the fighter;
And who made me Peninah, mother and wife;
And who made me Hannah, the blessed poetess.

Blessed be God, who made me a woman,
And who made me Naomi, strong and determined;
And who made me Ruth, faithful and courageous;
And who made me Hadassah, she is Esther, heroine of
    the Megillah;
And who made me Golda Meir, the brilliant leader.

At least once a day I look into the mirror that is in the
    room,
And in the mirror that is in the street, and I see "that it
    is good,"
And recite the blessing with pride:
Blessed be God, who made me a woman.

—Anonymous

Learn

When you have your period, it is a sign that you are healthy. The blood is a monthly reminder that your body is in harmony with life. You are young. In most cases your body now has the ability to become pregnant, something more appropriate when you are older and emotionally mature enough to be a parent.

Judaism makes many distinctions and separations between special things: Shabbat and the rest of the week, light and dark, holiness and the everyday, the time when menstrual blood is flowing and the time when it is not. In traditional Judaism, a woman is given three special time-bound mitzvot. One is lighting Shabbat candles (הדלקת נרות *hadlakat nerot*) 20 minutes before sundown. Another is tearing off a small chunk of dough and burning it when making *challah* for Shabbat (*hafrashat challah*–הפרשת חלה). The third is *niddah* (נידה), the mitzvah of a married woman going to a mikvah (ritual bath–מקוה) after her period. Together, the intials of these three activities form the word "Channah" (Challah, Niddah, Hadlakat Nerot–חנה=חלה, נידה, והדלקת נדות).

For many women, *mikvah* is a beautiful ritual, almost a spa experience, both physical and spiritual, wherein a woman recites blessings with each of three dunks, to celebrate and affirm her femininity and fertility. While once only practiced by traditional Jews, *mikvah* has been growing in popularity across the Jewish world. You may choose to observe this beautiful mitzvah if you get married.

Discuss

Did you, or will you, do anything special to mark your first period? There is an old Ashkenazi tradition of the "mazel tov slap," a symbolic smack on the cheek from Mom on the occasion of her daughter's first period, followed by a blessing for health and fertility. Some mothers and daughters go away for a weekend together. Some fathers give their daughters flowers. Perhaps you, your mother, and your friends could come up with your own way to make your first period into a meaningful event.

Pirkei Banot

"In the 21st century in the Western world, you hardly have to give a thought to your period—at least, compared to what girls and women had to deal with a century ago. Today there are pads, tampons, sponges, and painkillers to make the whole experience as convenient and comfortable as possible.

"However, it has also become invisible. I remember feeling a real letdown when the blood finally came. Most of my friends had already gotten their periods. I couldn't wait. But then nothing happened. No celebration, no marking of this life-changing occasion, no acknowledgment that I had just entered the worldwide community of adult women. There was only silence and a disappointing sense of invisibility.

"Many years later, in my 30s, I learned of a mitzvah that marked menstrual periods as part of a woman's life cycle. It was called 'going to the *mikvah* (מקווה).' At least there was something to mark my period. But it wasn't the same as if I had gone the very first time I got my period."

—Penina Adelman

Discuss

How does love figure into your close relationships? Are love and sex different aspects of the same thing? Do they mean an intimate relationship, or can they be totally separated? The most effective way to show you love someone is to give to him or her in a wholehearted way—physically, emotionally, intellectually, and spiritually. When you love another person, you want to give to him or her, to make them happy and feel good about themselves. You also want that person to give back to you, to know you in the deepest way, to validate you, to support you, and even to challenge you.

- What is your definition of love?
- Make a list of people you love. Why do you love each of them?
- Are there different kinds of love?
- Can we be obligated to love someone? *Ve'ahavta l'reyakha kamokha* (love your neighbor as yourself—ואהבת לרעך כמוך) is one of the most important and basic *mitzvot*. What does this mean to you?
- Do you believe in "love at first sight"?
- How do you show someone that you love him or her?

"My first kiss—I remember it like it was yesterday. [It was] the summer I was 14. He was 15. I had always had a crush on him; he was the cool guy at camp.... He asked me to the camp dance.... After the dance we had an hour before lights out. He asked me if I wanted to go to his cabin. When we walked in, no one was there. I suddenly got so nervous. I didn't understand what was going on, how I agreed to go to the cabin or what was going to happen. Although on the inside I was freaking out, I kept my cool on the outside. We sat on his bed looking at *Rolling Stone* magazine. I felt like he was moving closer to me. My palms began to sweat!... It was finally going to happen—my first kiss. He leaned towards me and looked me in the face and said, 'Tamara, you are really pretty, and I've had so much fun tonight with you. Can I kiss you goodnight?'... I looked at him, smiled, and said 'Yes!' He moved closer, his lips touched mine, and we kissed. Magic! Fireworks! My very first real kiss. It didn't last very long. I was a bit confused at first. But it was nice and sweet, and he was very gentle. We were both a bit uncomfortable after-wards, so he kind of just offered to walk me back to my cabin. When I walked through the door, all the girls wanted to know what happened. Although they were begging me to tell them, I really felt like this was something special that I wanted to keep to myself." —Tamara, 23

"I really don't [believe that] gay and straight girls are ultimately the same.... What's hard as a lesbian teenager, in particular a Jewish lesbian teenager, is not just the dating expectations but the constant sense of having to try to conform. [There is a] feel-ing of marginality, of having to prove yourself doubly as much as everyone else, of becoming more politically aware earlier, of being silenced.... I know that I learned about boundaries and transgression and facade much younger than most of my friends." —Aviva, 24

Sexual Safety

Once you recognize how sacred your body is, you respect its needs and desires. Others must respect it, too—that means respecting the boundaries you set. In earlier times (and today, still, in some cultures) women were totally dependent on men for their physical and sexual safety, economic stability, and social status, which made it possible to force women into having sex. In modern society, women are men's equals, and their sexual rights are protected under the law. They have the right of consent, which means that when you say, "No," it means NO.

◗ meet Dinah

The story of Dinah, Jacob's only daughter, illustrates the issue of rape and the position of women in the ancient world.

"Dinah, the daughter of Leah, whom she bore to Jacob, went out to see the daughters of the land. When Shechem, the son of Chamor the Hivite, a prince of the land, saw her, he took her, he lay with her, and he afflicted her" (Genesis 34:1–2). Like many a date rapist, Shechem then claims he is in "love" with her and starts to talk sweetly to her. We can only imagine how terrified Dinah must have been—literally, we must imagine, for Dinah's voice is never heard in the Torah. Her father and brothers do all the talking.

Shechem wants to marry Dinah, so his father, Chamor—whose name means "jackass" in Hebrew!—comes to Jacob to arrange a marriage.

In biblical times a woman was considered "damaged goods" if she was not a virgin when she was married. Thus, this would be the only chance Dinah would probably have to marry. Nevertheless, Jacob and his sons considered rape an "obscenity" (Genesis 34:7; נבלה–n'valah). Two of Dinah's brothers, Shimon and Levi, hatch a plot. They agree that Shechem may marry Dinah if all the men of his town, the Hivites, are circumcised. Chamor agrees to this; intermarriage with the Hebrews appeals to him because they are prosperous. However, as the men are recovering from their circumcisions, Shimon and Levi enter their town, slaughter them all, and rescue Dinah, who has been held captive at Chamor's palace.

Jacob is angry at his two sons for their excessive violence. "Shall he treat our sister like a whore?" they reply indignantly.

Discuss

- What do you think of the revenge taken by Dinah's brothers? If they had killed only the rapist and not all the men, would their action have been justified?
- What do you think Dinah was feeling and thinking? What would you have wanted to happen if you were she?
- Was the rape not really a rape, given that Shechem wanted to marry Dinah?

Learn

Now that you have met Dinah, let's discuss two Jewish concepts that can serve as a guide to taking control of your life before you get into a situation like hers.

One is *kavod habriot* (honoring all creatures–כבוד הבריות). Just as all creatures in this world are worthy of honor and respect, you too are worthy. Dinah was worthy, too. Fortunately, in our own time (at least in the Western world), a girl's honor and worth no longer depend on whether she is a virgin. Girls' reputations are still much more vulnerable than boys'. And the society we live in can often make it even more difficult for a teenage girl to resist early sexual involvement. Nevertheless, "no" means "no," and boys and men must respect your boundaries.

The other concept is *betzelem Elohim* (in the image of God–בצלם אלוהים). According to the Torah, we were all created in God's image, which means we all have a spark of God in us. Keeping this in mind, we are more likely to treat each other with honor, respect, and even a sense of awe. Animals were not created in the same image of God. Humans were instructed to behave in a more dignified way than animals do. This idea charges us with the responsibility to move beyond the physical and to look at each person with respect. We should be mindful to relate to humans as more than sexual, physical beings.

If you feel uncomfortable with the way another person is treating you and your body, it's important for you to speak up. Find an adult you can trust and tell her what is happening. Also, if someone you know is uncomfortable with the way another person is treating her or him, help this person speak up. Sexual coercion is a criminal act. However, even more subtle behaviors are reason enough to tell an adult. These include: touching inappropriately, pinching, cornering, writing sexual graffiti, making sexual jokes, spreading sexual rumors, pulling at someone's clothes or underwear, flashing or "mooning," forcing a kiss on someone, forcing someone to touch her or his private parts.

Pressure from a boyfriend or girlfriend should *never* make you feel guilty about refusing to do something you don't want to do, even though someone might try to persuade you by saying, "If you love me, you'll do it." In the 1950s, mothers would tell their daughters, "If he loves you, he'll wait." That advice is still true.

◗ Discuss

Having strong personal boundaries offers you a lifelong protection from all forms of exploitation. How do you protect yourself? Consider the following:

- Parents and other adults can help you to strengthen your personal boundaries by respecting your privacy and taking seriously your feelings and perceptions.
- Parents and other adults can damage your personal boundaries by turning to you to fill their emotional needs or by violating you physically or sexually.

- Learn to say NO. (In fact, learn to be assertive in saying YES and in saying NO!) It's good to try to make other people happy, but when your desire to please or your fear of disapproval is excessive, you may meet other people's needs at the expense of your own well-being and become an easy target for those who would use you. This thought is particularly relevant in the era of sexting and Instagram, when an innocent comment or picture can be used to shame someone.

- Learn to become more self-aware and set clear boundaries with other people. You can't be expected to serve another person always at the expense of your own needs. It's not healthy. You may have to enlist others to help you set limits for your own well-being.

- Practice saying no to others who might want to take advantage of you by doing role-plays with friends, teachers, parents. Take note when you see other people do this and learn from them.

- Understand that when your parents try to make sure you have adequate adult supervision in certain social situations with boys and girls together and try to enforce reasonable curfews, they are trying to lower the risk of dangerous sexual encounters.

Pirkei Banot

"When I was little, my parents always told me not to let anyone touch my private parts. I could recite their commandments verbatim. 'There are special parts of your body that no one is allowed to see or touch unless you let them. But don't let too many people see or touch them, because then they won't be special anymore.' Those rules didn't seem too hard to follow, but there was more to them than my parents realized. I didn't either, until one day in eighth grade.

"A friend of mind was going out with this guy. Over the weekend she went to his house: they kissed and took a selfie of it. A couple of weeks later she broke up with him. A few days after that, he posted the picture on the Internet and told everyone in our grade that she was a slut and 'easy.' At first my friend ignored this, but one day when I was walking down the hall with her, two guys screamed out to her, 'Hey, when did you become such a 'ho!' and called her a 'slut.'

"My friend began to cry. I hugged her and told her that they were being immature, but this incident was hard to ignore. It hurt both of us, because it was abusing her sexuality and exploiting it. This falls under the category of sexual harassment.

"The one thing my parents didn't include in their warnings was that words can be counted as sexual harassment, too! If someone has ever made you feel uncomfortable or embarrassed you about your sexuality, recognize immediately that it is wrong. Tell someone: a friend, a parent, or a teacher. Don't think that you are overreacting. It is your sexuality, it is a gift, and it deserves the utmost respect. Speak up!!" —Eliza, 17

Sexuality in Revolution

Is sex a private or a public thing—or both?

Sexuality is a natural human drive, like your appetite for food. As you mature into adolescence and beyond, you experience sexual desire, both physically and emotionally, and with varying degrees of intensity. As if that's not challenging enough, sexuality also has a powerful social component that for most people culminates in finding a partner, a significant other, with whom to share an intimate relationship.

Adolescence is a time when you develop all kinds of relationships from which you learn as much about yourself as you do about others. "Am I normal?"—That's a question adolescents frequently ask themselves. You can't help but look around at the world and its people and compare yourself to others. A healthy response requires good judgment and the ability to guard your own feelings and thoughts from the influential world of friends, family, and media. Try to allow yourself the freedom to acknowledge how you feel and what you think on the inside before you start factoring in others' opinions.

The world you live in is always in flux, but one dramatic change, the sexual revolution, began in the 1960s in the United States as a great cultural shift in politics, music, clothing, and self-expression. It became suddenly more acceptable to express a variety of social and sexual identities. Heterosexuality had been the norm for thousands of years, but over the decades that followed, many people began "coming out of the closet" to their friends and family, declaring their non-heterosexual identities as a matter of pride.

In 2015, the Supreme Court legalized gay marriage in the United States. No longer is same sex marriage a crime! Since then, there have been hundreds of cases involving gender choice and human rights and a growing understanding of a wide range of gender and sexual identities and expressions. LGBTQ (Lesbian, Gay, Bisexual, Trans, and Queer) is a movement demanding equality for all those who identify as non-heterosexual. Many heterosexual people support this movement and participate in gay pride activities. (Tel Aviv has one of the largest gay pride celebrations on the planet with more than 200,000 people from Israel and abroad attending a week of festivities and parade.)

Maybe you or some of your friends have already declared themselves non-cisgender (a different sex from what was recorded when they were born) or gay. Maybe you're confused by all the buzz around these subjects and the different ways people dress to express their differences. Some people want their own pronouns, others their privacy.

So sexuality—public or private? As they say, "it's complicated." The important thing for you, as you discover and express your own sexuality, is to not feel pushed or rushed into personal statements and behaviors you are not ready for. Life is long and judgment takes time to develop, especially while your hormones surge. Don't let social pressure disturb your developing sense of who you are and to whom you are attracted.

WRITE

A great exercise to discover your own inner thoughts and deep feelings is to find a prompt—whether a picture, an experience, or something you've read—and sit down and begin writing the first thing that comes to mind. Don't lift your pen from the page, or your fingers from the keyboard, and write. Don't worry about spelling or sentences. Don't judge. You're writing only for yourself. Just record as you let your consciousness flow freely with the random thoughts that fly through your mind. (Do not post this on the Internet!)

Do this several times. Try to get five or ten entries before reading them over. Then, as you read back over them, look for ideas and themes that repeat. This technique can bring you a powerful sense of your inner thoughts and better understanding of yourself. Just be sure to keep your writing in a safe place where privacy is assured.

Final Words

There is a French expression, "Plus ça change, plus c'est la même chose." It means "The more things change, the more they stay the same." That's a good way to explain the many changes in the latest phase of the sexual revolution. We are living at a time when gender definitions are becoming more fluid and individuals are free to express multiple ways of being a boy, a girl, a gay man, a lesbian woman, a transsexual, or something else. Many people now accept the notion that you can change your physical gender from what you were assigned at birth, whether through surgery or self-definition. Society is more open to adjectives that reflect unique self-concepts, individual choices in sexual partners, and lifestyles. There will always be people who identify non-traditionally and it is wonderful for society to finally allow people these basic freedoms. You can be who you feel you are—although sometimes it's not easy.

Sexuality should be healthy and pleasurable for all of us, no matter what our gender choices, as long as we feel in control of our own bodies and comfortable with our decisions. Being safe and up-to-date on information regarding protection from unwanted pregnancy and sexually transmitted diseases is a good way to be more comfortable and confident about your choices. Keep in mind that we do have to respect ourselves as our bodies grow and change. Part of what makes sexuality so special is being able to respect and appreciate someone else's body while that person does the same for you.

It is very important to realize that you, as a developing woman, are allowed to have sexual feelings. We women are allowed to want to be touched, to touch other people, and to touch our own bodies. As girls, we might only hear about boys wanting sex. But I assure you, it's so normal for us to feel the same way! Just like boys, we are starting to experience sexual feelings—we may be attracted to boys, girls, or both. Experimenting in ways that ensure your safety and comfort level is all part of growing up. So, learn about your body—learn what makes you feel good, learn your limits. And always respect yourself.

• •

Mitzvah–מצווה: Your shall not go as a talebearer among your people. Leviticus 19:6

לא תלך רכיל בעמך (ויקרא 19:16)

Learn–לימוד: watching your tongue–שמירת הלשון
Death and life are in the hands of language.–
המות והחיים ביד הלשון

• •

Thinking  Before I Speak

*I need to say what I feel and think, but
I may be hurting people when I do.*

Dear JGirl,

When I was in high school, I learned the hard way that name-calling can really hurt and harm people. The story I'm about to tell you has stuck with me all these years. I want to share it with you.

It was the ninth grade and all the girls thought the eleventh-grade boys were so cute. The guys liked us, too, because we were new to the school. After a while one guy, Alex, started hanging out with a friend of mine, who I'll call Amy. Soon he asked her to be his girlfriend. And she became the coolest girl in school, riding around in his car on the weekends with this "older" guy. He took her to parties with other juniors and to hang out with his older friends.

129

One Monday morning when I got to school, I heard a lot of whispering in the halls. I wasn't sure what happened. But when I got to my locker a friend came up to me and said, "Did you hear about Amy? She is such a slut! I can't believe what she did!" I innocently asked, "What did she do?" My friend answered, "She cheated on Alex with two different guys! He is devastated. He found out and broke up with her and is telling everyone what a slut she is." I was shocked. I thought Amy was a loyal friend and a really good person. I couldn't imagine why she would do something like that to her boyfriend.

When Amy came to school, she soon found that everyone was whispering about her. She walked down the hall when a bunch of eleventh-grade boys yelled out, "Hey guys, look at that slut strutting her stuff."

Amy left school immediately and didn't come back for days. When she returned, it took her weeks to smile again.

The truth soon surfaced. The story that was ruining Amy's life was a lie. Amy had not cheated on her boyfriend. He had pressured her to have sex with him and when she refused, he called her a tease. He fabricated the whole story to embarrass her. In reality, he was trying to intimidate her because he was scared he would get in trouble for being so aggressive. Unfortunately, people believed the guy and just gossiped about Amy.

Amy never got rid of her new nickname—"the Snow White slut." She is now very accomplished, married, and starting a family of her own. But still when people mention her, they remember her as "the Snow White slut," and she knows it.

It says in the Talmud that embarrassing someone is like murdering them. I never understood that until the situation with Amy happened. Rumors that defame someone's reputation do have the potential to "murder" someone. Before the rumors started, Amy felt like one girl. After the rumors, she felt like someone else. Hateful gossip is actually a sign of weakness, because the gossiper does not have the courage to say these words to the person's face.

In this chapter we will see how far the effects of negative speech can go. We'll also see how refraining from spreading rumors, sharing gossip, and engaging in lashon hara (לשון הרע) *will make us feel a lot happier.*

And remember, if you don't have something nice to say about someone, try not saying anything at all.

Good luck!
Ali

Guard Your Tongue (Psalm 34:14)

Learn

Let's talk about ways to watch your speech. The familiar meaning of *shmirat halashon* is "guarding your tongue" (שמירת הלשון)—that is, paying attention to everything you say and weighing whether it really needs to be said. Could your words possibly hurt someone's feelings, damage his reputation, diminish her self-esteem? Don't spread negative rumors.

In Jewish tradition, guarding your tongue means thinking before you speak, refraining from saying anything negative about another, telling the truth, being cautious about what you say, and considering how what you say could affect others. There are books and formulas with the goal of avoiding hurtful, negative kinds of talk. The Hebrew phrase for trash talk is *lashon hara* (literally, "evil speech"). One medieval rabbi (Orchot Tzaddikim) said that he who speaks *lashon hara* searches for people's flaws, like a fly who always lands in the dirtiest of places. One who speaks *lashon hara* disregards the good in people and focuses only on the bad. You should try to use skillful speech when you open your mouth—speech that helps and encourages people, strengthens relationships, and presents useful ideas.

TALK CAN GO VIRAL

Jewish girls and women have a lot to say. (They always have, even if it wasn't recorded for posterity.) That is why it is so important to watch over your speech—which includes your texting, posting, and instagramming—to be mindful of what you say. You have crucial things to say about Judaism and the Jewish People and the world. You may have important questions to ask. Yet in even the most insignificant small talk, we must be mindful of how we talk and what we say.

We all talk about other people. After all, we are only human. We also appreciate it when someone says something good about us, something that strengthens and affirms us.

The way you speak—and especially things that you circulate online—has a big impact on the people around you, and not always a positive one either. Often, you don't think much about what you're saying. You shoot off a text or forward someone else's and then forget about it. But once shared, that little photo or snippet of information is in the world forever. It can be retweeted and transformed, even ruin a person's life. Imagine being on the other end of an insensitive text or tweet. You might feel anything from mild embarrassment to fierce shame. When an individual or social group selects someone out for public criticism, that's bullying, a real crime for which people can be prosecuted. This may be difficult for some young people to understand until it happens to them, but texting or sexting is the surest way to lose one's privacy. An astute lawyer once said, "Don't write anything on paper or post anything to the Internet that you wouldn't want read aloud in a court of law."

Here are some examples of *lashon hara*:

- Derogatory statements, such as "Lexie said the stupidest thing in class today."
- Damaging statements, such as "I heard that Ella's parents are getting divorced because her mother cheated on her father" or "I heard that Stacey had stopped coming to dance practice because she is suffering from depression."
- Insulting statements: "Aliza's clothes look like hand-me-downs from her grandmother. How can she stand it?"

- Emphasizing undesirable traits: "Amy is so clumsy that I fear for my life whenever she's around."
- Belittling statements: "That new girl Zoe is so smart. You'd think she wouldn't even give Talya the time of day. I mean, Talya can hardly get a full sentence out, but they seem to like each other. Weird."
- False statements: "My father's client owns two seats at the sports stadium, and he promised me tickets to any concert I want to go to."

DON'T FORGET YOUR MOUTH GUARD

It's so easy to let your mouth run off. "She's a slut ... He's a loser ... It's so gay!" Guarding your speech takes discipline and understanding. You constantly put yourself in the frame of mind of the person you are going to talk about and remind yourself how hurt you would be if others were talking about you. Eliminating negative speech from your life is a challenge well worth undertaking.

It is important to note that reporting abuse is not *lashon hara*. Obviously, you must say something negative about the person who is hurting you. In this case, *Shmirat halashon* does not rule out talking to someone who can help you.

Outright lying and false testimony are forbidden by the ninth commandment. *Lashon hara* includes gossip as well as slander and libel, which means saying or writing something mean and untrue. Not only is it forbidden to speak *lashon hara,* it is forbidden to listen to it. You should walk away or even stop the speaker by saying you don't want to hear it.

Write

Can you think of examples of gossip or negative speech that you either said or heard? What made you say it? Did it have an impact on anyone else? What was your reaction when you heard it? Did you eagerly listen? Use your journal or blog to reflect on these times.

Rabbi Israel Meir Kagan, also known as the Chafetz Chaim ("he who loves life"), was famous for his ability to "guard his tongue." In the late 19th century he composed several important works that deal with the laws of *lashon hara* and strategies for fulfilling the mitzvah of *shmirat halashon* successfully. One of the methods he used is to request assistance from God. The following is one of his prayers:

> Gracious and merciful God, help me restrain myself from speaking or listening to derogatory, damaging, or hostile speech. I will try not to engage in *lashon hara,* either about individuals or about a group of people. I will strive not to say anything that contains falsehood, insincere flattery, scoffing, or elements of needless dispute, anger, arrogance, oppression, or embarrassment to others. Grant me the strength to say nothing unnecessary, so that all my actions and speech cultivate a love for Your creatures and for You.

What prayer would you write?

Learn

There is a Jewish folktale that illustrates the consequences of *lashon hara* with humor. It conveys a major point about *lashon hara:* You never know where your words might go (especially now with e-mail; someone you don't even know can access your words and use them in ways you never intended!). In Joan Rothenberg's retelling of this story, *Yettele Feathers,* the person guilty of *lashon hara* is a woman, although the Talmud's version of the story features a man.

> Once there was a woman who said awful things about another person. Realizing later how much she hurt this person, she went to her rabbi and asked, "Rabbi, what can I do?"

The rabbi thought a bit and told the woman to bring him a feather pillow. She brought the pillow and the rabbi said, "Now go outside, rip the pillow open, and shake out the feathers."

She did just that. As she was shaking out the feathers, the wind caught them, causing them to fly everywhere.

The woman returned to the rabbi and said, "I did as you told me. Now what?"

The wise man replied, "Now go back outside and pick up all the feathers."

The woman looked startled and said, "How can I? The wind took them! I don't even know where they are now."

The rabbi said, "Exactly. Just like your words. Once they're out, it's impossible to get them back."

m'korot

There are four biblical prohibitions that relate to *lashon hara*:

"Do not go talebearing among your people" (Leviticus 19:16). This is the commandment against being a gossip. If you have a problem with someone, you should talk to that person, not about the person to someone else. Or, you could do nothing at all and get over it.

"Do not carry false news" (Exodus 23:1). When you lie to others, God (and perhaps other people) ultimately knows the truth. Once you get caught in a lie, people begin to know you as a liar.

"You shall not curse the deaf or place a stumbling block before the blind" (Leviticus 19:14). This emphasizes how cruel it is to do something to someone who is unable to deal with it (for example, a deaf person can't hear the curse; a blind person can't see the stumbling block). This refers not only to people who have a physical disability; it can also apply to anyone with limitations of any sort: mental, social, academic, or physical. You should be careful about commenting on the limited abilities of others.

"You shall not take revenge or bear a grudge against your people, but you shall love your neighbor as yourself" (Leviticus 19:18). How many times have you been upset with a friend and not been able to confront that person? When the feelings are not released, the anger is buried and can turn into a long-term grudge and desire for revenge. Holding back one's anger can be a very difficult idea to live by. Just know that we all struggle with it at one time or another.

Discuss

What do these statements from the Book of Proverbs (King Solomon's wisdom) mean to you?

"One who goes talebearing reveals secrets, but one who is faithful of spirit conceals the matter." —Proverbs 11:13

"Pleasant words are like dripping honey, sweetness for the soul, and health for the bones." —Proverbs 16:24

"Death and life are in the power of the tongue." —Proverbs 18:21

Another idea that can help you stop yourself before saying something nasty about another person is thinking about what every Jew says on Yom Kippur. It's called the *Ashamnu* prayer. (*Ashamnu* means "we have sinned"–אשמנו). Let's look at the sins that the prayer assumes many of us engage in every year.

We abuse, we betray, we are cruel.
We destroy, we embitter, we falsify.
We gossip, we hate, we insult.
We jeer, we kill, we lie.
We mock, we neglect, we oppress.

We pervert, we quarrel, we rebel.
We steal, we transgress, we are unkind.
We are violent, we are wicked, we are xenophobic.
We yield to evil, we are zealous for bad causes.

What's interesting about this list is how many of the "sins" concern talking or speech. How many of them do you think can be related to *lashon hara*? Notice that betraying and gossiping are high up on the list, even before the terrible sin of killing. Jeering, killing, and lying are even on the same line! Some say that Judaism considers *lashon hara* the greatest sin.

When we say the *Ashamnu* prayer each year, we acknowledge that we do these things, and so should try to steer clear of them. It's great to start working on this now, avoiding these behaviors altogether or being as little involved with them as possible.

Next Yom Kippur, when you are in a synagogue, think about how you've done in resisting the temptation to engage in *lashon hara*.

How to combat *Lashon Hara*

- When you speak about someone to a third party, omit his or her name. It's a start!
- Before you speak, ask yourself if what you are saying is true. If not, close your mouth or else you'll become known as a liar.
- Ask yourself why you feel the need to speak negatively about someone. Are you angry at him or her? Are you insecure about something? Think about it before you open your mouth and let the words jump out.
- Ask yourself, "Are my words going to harm anyone?" and "How would I feel if someone were talking that way about me?"
- Refrain from jokes that insult others. As Jews, we have often been hurt by anti-Semitic humor.

- When others start to gossip, leave the room. (If you have the courage, object to what is being said.) Just because everyone is doing it, doesn't mean that you have to join them.
- Stay away from people who constantly engage in *lashon hara*. Bad behavior has a way of rubbing off on others.

When writing or answering an email, always make sure the address section is blank until you have finished writing. That way you won't accidentally send something unintended. Taking a deep breath and being sure you mean to say what you do can save many embarrassments.

Pirkei Banot

"I know a girl who tries so hard not to gossip. Every night before she goes to bed she reads this tiny book of reminders on not to spread gossip. She also always writes in her journal if she is really frustrated with someone or has a secret to share. I asked her once why she was so good at not spreading gossip. She told me that when she was younger, someone spread a terrible lie about her. Ever since then, she vowed to watch what she says!"
—Nicole, 14

"Many girls are mean to each other.... They talk behind each other's backs, tell secrets, exclude, and do many other harsh things. Perhaps girls are jealous.... Many girls in my grade are rich and buy expensive clothing. Every day at school, they look each other up and down to see what they are wearing. Lots of girls feel better about themselves when they don't like what someone else is wearing. Another issue among girls is lack of trust. When your so-called best friend talks about you behind your back, you feel as if you can't trust her anymore. But the thing I hate the most is exclusion. I have been in so many situations where I have been excluded even by my good

friends. Most of my friends gossip, talk about each other behind their backs, exclude, and do other things that would qualify as rude behavior. I think that girls should be supportive and caring. No one is better than anybody else. What is the point of commenting negatively about someone? In many cases, the mean girls are the ones who are popular, but that shouldn't be the case. We should all learn to love each other and be nice to one another."
—Ariela, 13

"I had a teacher in the sixth grade who knew how to make me feel good. She had a saying that made me feel like I could take on the world: 'You should be so proud of yourself.' After working almost a month on a nature project, I was very nervous about presenting it to the class. I had done the research and the work, but I had to talk about it in French! At the end of the presentation, everyone applauded, but I still wasn't sure how I was feeling…. After the class when the bell rang, Mrs. Levy put her arm around me and said, 'You should be very proud of yourself.' She was right! It was then that I realized that no matter what anyone else thought, I had worked hard and accomplished something I had never done before. She made sure I understood that her approval wasn't the issue, that I had to feel good about it for myself."
—Lisa, 25

The Consequences of Gossip

◖meet◗ Miriam the Prophet

One of the most prominent women in the Torah is Miriam, the sister of Moses and Aaron. Together the three of them led the Jewish People out of Egypt by using the strengths with which each had been blessed by God.

Miriam was a young girl when Pharaoh, the ruler of Egypt, declared that all Jewish boys were to be killed at birth. Many Jewish men thus began divorcing their wives to prevent the births and subsequent deaths of sons. Miriam's father, Amram, grew increasingly fearful and told his wife, Yocheved, that he had to divorce her for this reason.

Miriam approached her father and explained to him that what he was doing was worse than Pharaoh's decree. She said, "*Abba* [father], don't you realize that if you divorce *Ima* [mother] in order to prevent the birth of boys, you are also preventing the birth of girls?" Considering Miriam's words, Amram returned to his wife. Other Jewish men followed his example and returned to their wives as well.

After Moses was born, Miriam had the idea to stand on the bank of the Nile River and watch what would happen to her baby brother when Yocheved placed him in a basket in the river to escape Pharaoh's decree. Miriam then cleverly suggested to Pharaoh's daughter, who found the baby and decided to adopt him, that she bring a Hebrew nursemaid for him. Pharaoh's daughter agreed, and Miriam brought her own mother to take care of her own baby!

When the Jews were finally freed from slavery, Miriam led the women in singing and dancing when they reached the other side of the Sea of Reeds. The Midrash says that during the forty years in the wilderness, water was provided to the Jews from a well that traveled with Miriam. This idea is based on an unexplained sequence of events in the Torah: As soon as Miriam dies, the Jews have a serious water shortage (Numbers 20:1–2).

Miriam's every action was not positive, however. A major story about her concerns *lashon hara*.

"Miriam and Aaron spoke against Moses because of the Cushite woman he had married.... 'Has *Adonai* spoken only to Moses? Doesn't *Adonai* also speak to us?' *Adonai* heard it. Moses was very humble, more so than all the people on the face of the earth" (Numbers 12:1–3).

Miriam, who initiated the conversation criticizing Moses and his choice of a wife, is punished by God with a skin disease, *tzara'at* (צרעת–often mistranslated as "leprosy"). As a result, she has to be confined outside the camp for a week. During this time, the entire camp of the Israelites comes to a grinding halt—testimony to her importance. Only after the week was up could the Jews begin to travel again.

Aaron, the "listener" of the *lashon hara,* is not punished with the disease, only with the horror and fear one has when a loved one is deathly ill. This consequence might be seen as an even greater punishment than having the disease itself. Aaron's punishment was passive because his involvement in the *lashon hara* was passive: He listened and did not object.

The Midrash suggests that Miriam was actually speaking out of sympathy for Moses' wife, Zipporah, whom Moses was ignoring because he was always up on Mt. Sinai talking to God! Miriam was saying, in effect, "We're prophets, too, but we don't ignore *our* spouses!

Discuss

- What do you make of this story?
- Do you think it was fair to punish Miriam actively and Aaron passively? Why or why not?
- Try taking Miriam's point of view and imagine how she must have felt during those seven days when she was confined.
- Do you think Miriam thought God was being "unfair"? Have you ever been singled out for a punishment that you thought was unfair? Have you ever seen this happen to someone else?
- Does the fact that Miriam may have had good intentions—her concern for Zipporah—make a difference? Have you ever badmouthed someone out of concern for that person's possible mistreatment of another?

meet Michelle Carter the Cyber Bully

In June of 2017, a Massachusetts court convicted Michelle Carter of involuntary manslaughter in the 2014 death of her friend, Conrad Roy. Roy and Carter had met online five years earlier and communicated with each other in texts and by phone. Roy was an introspective person, somewhat anxious and depressed, but was seeing a therapist and taking an anti-depressant. Carter had been, for most of their relationship, a supportive friend to the socially awkward teen. She had often encouraged Conrad to seek treatment for his problems.

Prosecutors depicted Carter as someone who liked the attention she received when telling friends about her "suicidal boyfriend." She even sent texts to girls she wanted to befriend, pretending that Roy was missing, so that she could get their sympathy and attention. Then, eleven days before his death by suicide, Carter began sharing research and ideas about suicide with Roy. Although she wasn't physically present when he took his own life, she did urge him, in texts and, finally, by phone, to get back in his truck and asphyxiate himself.

That night, after Roy's suicide, Carter texted a friend "… his death is my fault like honestly I could have stopped him I was on the phone with him and he got out of the car because it wasn't working and he got scared and I f—ing told him to get back in…." Michelle Carter was convicted of third degree manslaughter in Conrad Roy's death. As the Judge recounted in his verdict, he indicated Carter had caused a dangerous environment with her encouragement of suicide and had a duty to save him if she could. Judge Moniz said "… he exited the truck—he literally sought fresh air…. (And then Carter) "She instructs him to get back into the truck, well knowing of the feelings he has exchanged … his ambiguities, his fears, his concerns."

Most cyberbullying does not go this far. But all of it can cause "mini-deaths": damage to reputation, to self-worth, and personal dignity.

DISCUSS

Share your thoughts about this story. Does it make any difference that Conrad Roy had made a previous attempt at suicide or that Michelle Carter was also taking an anti-depressant and unstable?

Genesis contains the story of Adam and Eve's sons, Cain and Abel. Cain killed Abel, his brother, and when God asks Cain where his brother is, Cain responds, "Am I my brother's keeper?" The rabbis explain that God's punishment of Cain is a recognition that all humans are related to and responsible, one for the other. Do you think this value stands behind the judge's verdict in Michelle Carter's case? Do you agree with the verdict?

Language has overwhelming power, both for good and evil. What can you do with your communication to create a positive effect in the real and cyber world?

Silence

Silence is many-sided. On the one hand, silence may incorrectly signify the absence of important speech—such as the lack of a written record of the Jewish women's talk over the centuries. On the other hand, silence can be a strong force for good. Shimon, the son of Rabban Gamliel, said, "All my life I have been raised among the sages, and I have not found anything better for oneself than silence" (*Pirkei Avot* 1:17).

Silence is a way to get in touch with the innermost parts of one's being. It can be difficult, but silence sometimes may be what your soul needs in order to thrive. Can you think of times this has been true for you? Can you imagine times it might have been true for others? Certainly when someone wants to pick a fight, it can be really helpful to say very little—or nothing at all.

Final Words

"Words should be weighed, not counted" is an old Yiddish expression. This is true when you are speaking to your friends, teachers, and family. It is also true for yourself. Think about the words you use in describing yourself, your looks, your feelings, your dreams, your conflicts. Be good to yourself in choosing words wisely. A well-chosen word is like a jewel fitting right into its setting.

As a Jewish girl living today, you are fortunate to have more and more words available from women of the past. You can learn what your ancestors were doing, thinking, and feeling. You can see how different and how similar you are from them. Most of all, the voices of Jewish women today are ringing out in ways that will be recorded for posterity.

Rabbi Sheila Shulman of the Leo Baeck Institute in London believes that Jewish women and girls are prophets nowadays and even predicting the future. Prophets are people who have always told the truth, describing the world as they see it to the best of their abilities. To say that women and girls are in a "prophetic position" means that we have the potential of saying what it is to be Jewish and whole and fully female and human. As a bat mitzvah, you are finding your voice as a Jewish woman and as a member of the human race. May you learn to take responsibility for your words. May you find your deepest, truest voice and speak proudly in the world.

Mitzvot: *Tikkun olam* (repairing the world– תיקון עולם)
Kol Yisrael areivim zeh bazeh (all of Israel are responsible for one
another) כל ישראל ערבים זה בזה

Getting Involved

*I want to make the world
a better place, but there
are just too many problems.*

Dear JGirl,

I grew up in the turbulent 1960s, when students protested the Vietnam War and committed themselves to becoming a generation of change. You may be growing up in equally turbulent times. We had the assassination of John F. Kennedy, Robert Kennedy, Martin Luther King Jr., and the birth of TV news that provided graphic images of war and suffering. You've had to become accustomed to frequent mass shootings and terrorism on a larger international scale. Your world, since 9/11, has become increasingly violent and insecure, threatened by climate change and political upheaval. The pervasive presence of screens cry out for your attention.

At the same time, your world has evolved into an interactive Wonderland where people and continents are connected by easy travel and the immediacy of the Internet. With interconnectivity, people actively engage with each other solving shared problems, thus moving knowledge and understanding forward like never before. Building on each others'

145

discoveries and accomplishments, we 21st-century citizens have become the most collaborative group the world has ever seen. And that leaves you with a lot of opportunity to do good in the world, for yourself and others.

Will your generation take a more spiritual and activist path as well? Already we have seen millennials develop into a more tolerant and open-minded generation, working to save the environment and elevate human rights. Young people have become increasingly active in movements to defend marriage equality, secure women's rights, eradicate poverty, and put an end to gun violence. And spiritually? We hope Judaism will become an answer to your spiritual quest, since it offers values and practices with which you can make your life more meaningful and achieve these high goals.

Because it draws on our common humanity and creates positive results in the world, tikkun olam—*literally, "repairing the world"—has come to represent one of Judaism's best-known mitzvot. Whether applied to specifically Jewish problems or those in the greater community, this powerful concept does move us to create a better world.* Tikkun olam *has evolved as a popular motivation for Jews to work for social justice and the improvement of life on this planet. It is a core Jewish value that wherever you are, you should try to improve things, both in the Jewish community and in the larger world.*

Still, sometimes we and the people closest to us need to work first on fixing ourselves. This is another meaning of Kol k'vodah bat melekh p'nimah—*that is, the inner work must go on alongside the outer work. Thoughtfulness about what we need to improve inside ourselves is essential if we want to improve anything outside ourselves. We must keep going from inside to outside and back again to work on the transformation of our whole planet.*

In the United States, a spirit of volunteering for the sake of the community—whether that is your neighborhood, your school, or your temple or synagogue—has been on the rise since September 11, 2001. Throughout the United States and Canada, people are working on food drives for the hungry and for organizations that build houses for people who need them. Some congregations are adopting refugee families and addressing problems facing America's newest immigrants.

As it says in Pirkei Avot *2:21, "It is not your duty to complete the work, but neither are you free to desist from it."*

B'hatzlachah!

Best of Luck!

Ellen

Make A Difference

Whether you are an Orthodox, Conservative, Reconstructionist, Reform, or a secular Jew, *tikkun olam* is an important Jewish obligation. We must find ways to make the world better, to help others in need, and to find even the smallest way to improve the world's troubles. It is difficult in this materialistic, self-centered Western world to maintain a sense of responsibility for your neighbor, let alone the rest of the world. While *tikkun olam* can mean saving the whales, the rain forest, and feeding all the starving children in Ethiopia, it also includes the many small acts of kindness you do every day at home.

According to the Bible, God created the world as a place for people to live. With the privilege of living here also comes the responsibility to care for it. In Jewish belief, every action counts, and every individual has the ability to change the world. As partners with God, it is a Jew's mission to fix things on earth that have become broken. The Talmud (*Sanhedrin* 27b) says, *Kol Yisrael areivim zeh bazeh* (all of Israel are responsible for one another). This means that every Jew must be attentive to every other Jew's needs. It's similar to saying, "Take care of yourself and your family first and then the rest of the world," because all Jews are "family." It also means that whatever one Jew does reflects upon all other Jews. Today, when there is a great deal of anti-Semitism, or hatred of Jews, and the State of Israel is so threatened, all Jews are particularly accountable for one another's actions. Our actions must be thoughtful and positive.

What are the internal Jewish directions that *tikkun olam* might take? The classic example is adding an extra mitzvah to your routine, perhaps taking particular care with *lashon hara* or learning Hebrew. A more outer-directed Jewish commitment might be standing up for Jews where and when they are threatened. The thousands of Jews worldwide who committed to saving Soviet Jewry by bringing Russian Jews to Israel and the United States in the 1960s and '70s were practicing *tikkun olam*. They were very successful in an enormous undertaking. Don't be afraid of challenges such as these.

Perhaps you will choose to stand up for Israel and Zionism against anti-Semitic slurs, using facts and *hasbara* (הסברה) to help explain Israel's position in the world. Whether you commit yourself to a program of Jewish learning or become an active Jewish feminist, your practice of *tikkun olam* for the benefit of the Jewish People is an important contribution bound to enhance your growth into womanhood. Supporting Israel is also a great example of *tikkun olam*.

It is a good habit to be involved in *tikkun olam* projects in both the Jewish world and the larger, secular world. We know this from the saying of Rabbi Hillel in the Talmud: "If I am not for myself, who will be for me? But if I am only for myself, what am I?" (*Pirkei Avot* 1:14).

Write

Take a big piece of paper and draw four concentric circles on it with lots of space between each one. Then fill in the circles according to the following:

Outer circle: World problems
First inner circle: Your country's problems
Second inner circle: Jewish People's problems
Innermost circle: Your personal problems

Now take a look at the *New York Times* or your city's daily newspaper. Read five or six articles about a world crisis: Israel's survival, war, starving children, disease, drought. Then write down in your journal or blog the problems that they pinpoint.

Which problem, from these articles or from other crises you are aware of in the world, do you wish you could fix? How would you go about fixing that problem? Which problem in your country do you wish you could fix? Which problem of the Jewish People do you wish you could fix? Finally, which problem in yourself do you wish you could fix? Take some time to reflect on this and use your journal to come up with some ways you could do *tikkun olam* for each of the circles. Do you see how *tikkun olam* relates to all the other mitzvot?

Discuss

Once, while Moses ... was tending his father-in-law Jethro's flocks, one of the kids ran away. Moses ran after it until he reached a small, shaded place. There, the small goat came across a pool and began to drink. As Moses approached it, he said, "I did not know you ran away because you were thirsty. You are so exhausted!" He then put it on his shoulders and carried it back. God said, "Since you tend the flocks of human beings with such overwhelming love—by your life, I swear you shall be the shepherd of My own flock, Israel." —*Exodus Rabbah* 2:2

What do you think about this way of choosing a leader for the Jewish People? How would you choose a leader? Compare with the way in which Rebecca was chosen by Eliezer (see chapter 2).

m'korot

"One who saves a Jewish life is considered as if he/she has saved the entire world." —Talmud, *Sanhedrin* 37a

Hillel said, "If I am not for myself, who will be for me? But if I am only for myself, what am I? And if not now, when?" —*Pirkei Avot* 1:14

"Give to the poor, Jew and non-Jew alike, and thereby bring peace to the world." —Talmud, *Gittin* 61a

"Upon three things the world stands: Torah, divine service, and deeds of lovingkindness." —*Pirkei Avot* 1:2

Putting the World Back Together

Four centuries ago in Safed, a city in Israel that was the center of Jewish mysticism in medieval times, there lived Rabbi Isaac Luria, better known as "the Ari." He would hear about events in the world and wonder how God could allow so many people to suffer so many injustices. He didn't think that people deserved all the suffering they experienced.

After the Ari thought about this for a long time, he had an insight. He believed that when God finished creating the world, God decided to pour a jar of peaceful, loving light onto it as a finishing touch. As the light was pouring out, the jar suddenly exploded into a million pieces. People suffer today because pieces of that light are scattered throughout the world. In order to put an end to the suffering, all of the pieces must be joined back together.

The rabbi was saddened by this thought. How were the Jews supposed to reconstruct a million pieces? It is hard enough putting a jigsaw puzzle together, let alone collecting a million pieces of love, peace, and light. The Ari considered the problem. If people start acting in a peaceful, loving way toward one another, perhaps those pieces of love and peace could reattach themselves.

The Ari then held a town meeting to present his ideas. The community was receptive and all were inspired to change their behavior. He explained to them that by trying to instill more love, order, and peace in this world, we can cause the pieces to re-form. As Jews, one of the most important tasks in life is to find what is broken in this world and repair it. By trying to fix what is broken, saving others from pain and lending a helping hand when in need, we are fulfilling our role as menders of the world.

Do It

Volunteering your time and energy is a crucial part of *tikkun olam*. Call your city government to find out who is in charge of volunteer services or community service. Contact that person and get a list. You can also do this with your school or local synagogue or Jewish Family Services. Go online to discover the websites of some truly amazing Jewish foundations and projects.

Here are some ideas:

- Visit a seniors' home. The holidays are an especially lonely time for many people, especially senior citizens who are confined to a nursing home. Get together a group of your friends and go to a nursing home. You have such power to bring joy to them by being with them, listening to them, singing to them, telling stories, and bringing them holiday treats. You can organize this with the local Jewish nursing home close to a holiday.
- Beautify a park. Contact the person or department responsible for parks and recreation in your community to find ways you can beautify your public spaces. You could plant flowers or clean up a local park.
- Assist with Passover preparation. Passover is one of the most stressful times all year because of the enormous amount of preparation involved. Perhaps in your community there are families who need help with this. Assistance can range from entertaining children to helping an adult cook to scrubbing kitchen cabinets.
- Plant trees in Israel. Helping the Land of Israel to grow is a way to honor friends and relatives for specific occasions or to remember friends and relatives who have passed away. Also, consider planting trees in Israel in honor of your guests instead of buying elaborate centerpieces of flowers or giving out bags of candy at your bat mitzvah party.

- Install a food barrel in your local synagogue or other Jewish communal building. Collect food and distribute to people in need, either through local agencies or individual contacts.

- Make a *tzedakah* box for your home. Commit to making a donation every Friday evening before blessing the candles. When it is full, have the entire family decide where the money should go.

- Clothe the needy. Sort through your closet and make a pile of clothing you can donate to a place that accepts used clothing for needy people. By doing this you will be performing the mitzvah of *halbashat arumim* (הלבשת ערומים– clothing the naked).

- Commit to studying the *parasha* each week, whether in a group or privately, by reading some of the great sources that are available to you online.

- Choose one day of the week to be your *tikkun olam* day. Make sure you try to "fix the world" in at least two ways, from small things like smiling at the bus driver or saying thanks to your teacher to larger efforts such as helping to make dinner or spending time with a disabled person. Every action makes a difference.

Pirkei Banot

"In the past, I've done a variety of things. I was part of the leadership team when I was in middle school. We did many projects, such as collecting books to give to people less fortunate, reading books to second graders in the poorer part of Boston, making sandwiches and cupcakes for shelters, and helping animals in need. It made me feel good to do this service, and I know that the people (and animals!) we were helping were very grateful." —Jessie, 15

◯ Learn

It was young Jewish women in their teens or early 20s, Yiddish-speaking immigrants, who sparked the first general strike of the garment industry.... They were amazing, those tireless, fearless cap-makers, button-makers, waistmakers, corset-makers, and cloakmakers. After long days in brutal working conditions, they organized, preached, rallied, marched.... Singed by exclusion from every side, yet deeply loyal to their ethnicity and to the working class, young women like Clara Lemlich, Paula Newman, Rose Schneiderman and Fannia Cohn defied the male leaders and organized from the grassroots up....They fought with equal fervor for better wages and for education, culture and a more humane way of life....

The housewives were activists, too.... Speechifying to crowds of women from their tenement windows, [they] organized strikes against high-priced kosher butchers and gouging land-lords. And it was Lillian Wald, a pioneering social worker at the time, who invented the concept of rent control.

I'm proud to note that Jewish women have made stellar contributions to the modern women's movement, too—Betty Friedan, author of the 1963 groundbreaking work *The Feminine Mystique*, ... Phyllis Chesler, feminist psychologist and writer, Bella Abzug, social activist and politician, and scores of other speakers, organizers, writers and grassroots activists ... we share in the prophetic tradition of idealism and in the outsiders' perspective. —Michele Landsberg, columnist for the *Toronto Star*

◯ Learn   SPEAK (AND WRITE) THE TRUTH

In 1993, historian Deborah Lipstadt, a professor at Emory University, published *Denying the Holocaust: The growing assault on truth and The Growing Assault on Truth and Memory,* a book about people who claim that the Holocaust did not happen. One such person she describes is another historian, David Irving, a British man who did not accept the physical evidence that is available in archives and museums or the testimony of thousands of Jewish eyewitnesses who survived the concentration camp at Auschwitz.

In his numerous books, David Irving made outrageous statements. One was that Adolf Hitler was "the biggest friend the Jews had in the Third Reich." Irving said that if Hitler had not helped the Jews, they would never have been able to create the State of Israel. In his writing and speeches, Irving called the Holocaust a hoax created by a worldwide secret Jewish group as part of its sinister plan to rule the world. Enraged by Lipstadt's assertions that he was a "Holocaust denier" and an unprofessional historian, Irving sued her for libel in a British court of law. Ultimately, after a hard-fought legal battle, David Irving was completely discredited. The court found that Lipstadt had indeed told the truth: Irving was a Holocaust denier, an anti-Semite, a racist, and a bad historian who had deliberately manipulated and falsified historical evidence.

For Lipstadt, winning the case was not enough. It was following the trial, in 2006, that Professor Lipstadt wrote, *Denying the Holocaust*, a powerful documentation of her experience in the trial. In 2016, her book was made into the popular film *Denial*, starring Rachel Weiss in the role of Deborah Lipstadt. (It's worth seeing!) "David Irving knew the truth," Lipstadt told interviewers. "He knew what the documents said, but he took the documents...and he changed, rewrote, omitted, reversed." This made his work a body of lies.

Many times in your life, you will come upon lies, distortions of the truth, and falsehoods that malign or injure people. How will you respond? Will you have the courage and determination of a Deborah Lipstadt? Most people do not have the courage to stand up for the truth. That's why Deborah Lipstadt is a heroine.

Nevertheless, it is important to know that Deborah did not act alone. As soon as she declared herself ready to fight, many people came to her side and supported her. You can do that, as well. You can help someone—anyone—who is standing up to lies. This also takes courage.

◯ meet Women Who Are Making a Difference in Jerusalem

- Michal Belzberg, at 13, canceled her lavish bat mitzvah party because of all the terrorism that was happening in Israel. She and her family initiated an organization called One Family (www.onefamily.org.il), which helps families who are victims of terrorism.
- Matan Daniel, who at 17 took on the cause of Israeli MIAs (soldiers who are missing in action). She educates people about what they can do to put pressure on the governments and help the families of the MIAs.
- Sarah Miran started a recycling program.
- Minna Wolf, 32, initiated an Israeli junior girls' baseball league.
- Barbara Bloom Silverman created "Package from Home," a program that sends food and presents to support Israeli soldiers.
- Alice Shalvi, an Israeli professor and feminist, helped bring progressive education to girls and elevated the status of women.
- Women of the Wall, founded in 1988, came together to demand women's rights to pray publicly at the Western Wall in Jerusalem. For 30 years, activists like Anat Hoffman have faced arrest and abuse for holding minyanim at the Wall (know in Hebrew as the Kotel–כותל), while petitioning the Israeli Supreme Court for equal treatment under the law.

And, Speaking of Israel …

Israel and Zionism

Zionism is the dream, and now reality, of the Jewish people returning to their homeland after thousands of years in exile, dispersed among the nations of the world. Without our own country and during times of persecution, the Jewish people suffered enormously. As recently as World War II, a third of all world Jewry was murdered: 6,000,000 people, including 1.5 million children.

Although some Jews remained in the Biblical land of Israel since the Babylonian exile, they had no political rights. It was the founding of the State of Israel in 1948 as an independent Jewish democracy that gave us, at long last, a safe haven from persecution. The State of Israel has absorbed millions of Jewish refugees who survived the Holocaust, from hostile Arab countries, and from world-wide anti-Semitism. Freedom to live as a Jew in the world, to observe Shabbat, speak our own language, and not be attacked by anti-Semites, though it seems a given when you're born into it, is still a relatively new and unique blessing.

Over the decades, Israel has been dragged into wars with its hostile Arab and Muslim neighbors, all of whom have denied its right to exist. As a result of its success in the 1967 war, Israel acquired control over the West Bank and East Jerusalem, land that had been part of Biblical Israel but that had most recently been ruled by Syria and Jordan. (Israel also acquired the entire Sinai Peninsula, but returned it to Egypt in exchange for peace.) The millions of Arabs that live in those places have become known as the Palestinians and, unwilling to accept Israeli governance, they have developed as an insurgency demanding statehood with increasingly violent expressions of nationalism.

Many Arab leaders haven't helped to end this situation, blaming Israel for their plight and attempting to destroy the Jewish State. That's why Israel was the first country to experience Radical Islamic terrorism. Unable to find a partner in peace among the Arab leadership, Israel continued to rule these territories and thus has earned the reputation of "occupier." Meanwhile, the two peoples, the children of Israel and the children of Ishmael, continue their tragic drama on the world stage. "Making peace in the

Middle East" has become a problem so intractable that the phrase is widely used to mean "accomplishing the impossible."

Speaking of the impossible, Israel is one of the youngest countries in the world, the only democracy in the Middle East, and one of the most diverse, pluralistic, multi-cultural places on earth. The young, vibrant, and thriving country is a modern miracle known internationally as a "start-up nation." You can thank Israel for the chip in your cell phone and computer, for Waze, the genius crowdsourced navigation app, and for so many of the advances it's brought about in medicine, technology, and even farming.

Unfortunately, anti-Semitism did not end with the establishment of Israel in 1948. And no matter what its politics, whether right or wrong, Israel has become the object of criticism, protests, incitement, and terror. Nevertheless, Israel remains the homeland of the Jewish people and the home of its Arab, Christian, Druze, and Bedouin citizens. Maybe you will be fortunate enough to travel to Israel with your family or on a birthright trip. Perhaps you'll sign up for a program to study or work or do an archaeological dig. Maybe, using Jewish genealogical searches, you will find and reconnect with a branch of your family now living there. Whatever your route, be sure to visit Israel and enjoy the modern miracle of our Jewish homeland.

◖DO IT

No matter what your connection, helping Israel is a great way to practice *tikkun olam* and to get to know more about your Jewish roots and Zionism.

Read books. Go to lectures. Educate yourself about Israel. Take advantage of the rich online presence of our Jewish state. (But in your online travels, beware of unbalanced news and Photoshopped images badmouthing Zionism.)

Follow news of BDS (an economic tool using Boycott, Divest, and Sanctions) and other systematic plans to defame Israel and incite violence against Jewish people. Contact leaders in your Jewish community and find a way to help.

Pirkei Banot

"In about a year and half I will serve in the army like every other girl in Israel who reaches the age of 18. In Israel you don't need something specific that will push you to be in *Tzahal* (צה"ל–צבא להגנה לישראל), the Israeli army, because we know, and people keep reminding us, that we have no other choice. I know that I have no other country in the world that I can call home besides Israel, and because of that I will give two years of my life for the country, the Israeli people, and all the Jews around the world, so that they'll have a home in Israel.

"Here in Israel, serving in the army is obvious. We live in a reality in which every day we hear about *Tzahal*'s actions, and we always know that one day it will be us who will need to protect the country. I can say that every child in Israel just knows that.

"And now to you girls around the world...: If you feel as I do that there's no other home like Israel and you feel that there's some kind of a bond between you and your Jewish brothers and sisters in Israel and you want to help them, come and join us in our home and give your best to the country. You can do that by serving in the army, do a *sherut leumi* (שירות לעומי–national service, like AmeriCorps) or just *make aliyah* (עליה–immigrate to Israel).

"I'm a 17-year-old girl from Jerusalem, not religious at all, and basically do stuff just like all of you around the world. Hope to see you all in Israel in the future!" —Matan Daniel, 17

meet Queen Esther

The story of Esther is one of many people's favorite parts in the Bible. It's got everything—suspense, mystery, drama, and a beautiful Jewish woman who is courageous and saves her people from the wicked Haman.

Actually, Esther is not unique. In fact, most of the women of the Bible are courageous. But Esther is special: A whole *megillah* (מגילה), or scroll, is devoted to her, as is the holiday of Purim.

When Esther was a girl, she was forced to leave her family and was taken to a place where she did not know the language and where she was made to live in a harem to serve the king's needs. She was compelled to become the queen of a king who spent most of his time giving lavish banquets. Because Esther was so young (maybe your age!) when her story began, she really needed to lean on someone who could guide her. That person was Mordechai, her uncle. Under his tutoring and with her new experiences in the royal court, she became mature.

Esther is a heroine for many reasons. She was smart and clever, throwing parties to trick Haman, and even though she's known for her beauty, it is her bravery that we celebrate each year. With a full belief in God, and after a period of intensive concentration through fasting, she decided to risk her life by confronting the king with truth. You know the rest of the story.

Very few people in those ancient days—or now—have the courage to challenge someone who is in a position of power and speak up for what they know is right the way Esther did.

◖meet Alicia Silverstone

Alicia, an animal rights and environmental activist, vegan, nutrition writer, and movie star, was born in San Francisco in 1976. She grew up with a passion for performing, acting in her first play when she was three, and modeling by age eight. As an adolescent she had a career built on her beauty, but she maintains a no-nudity policy in all her acting. After appearing in *Crush* (1993) and the Aerosmith video *Cryin'* (1994), she achieved success as a comic actress in *Clueless* (1995). Her success was short-lived, however, as a result of the low ratings of her next two movies, *Batman* (1996) and *Excess Baggage* (1997). Following this disappointment, she gained weight and became a joke to many actors in

Hollywood. Nevertheless, she challenged them all with an undaunted spirit, courage, and Jewish faith. Her career recovered and she went on to appear in many movies, TV, and music videos for which she received Emmy, Golden Globe, and MTV awards.

Alicia is a member of numerous animal rights organizations, including the Ark Trust and Last Chance for Animals. She endorses PETA, sends out pro-animal literature in her fan mail, and volunteers for animal groups.

Jewish tradition was always important to Alicia's family. Her father encouraged his wife and children to light Shabbat candles and make the blessing over the *challah*. From ages 5 through 13 Alicia studied Judaism three times a week. "I was reared in a traditional Jewish household," she says. "We lit candles Friday night and had seders. I and my brother David went to Hebrew school and had our bar and bat mitzvahs. I have wonderful memories of my bat mitzvah." Alicia says she still holds Jewish tradition dear to her. "Sitting in synagogue, singing songs, it's a very close, warm feeling. I feel that religion is in your heart."

meet Bella Abzug

Bella Abzug, a U.S. congresswoman for six years (1970–1976), was born in the Bronx on July 24, 1920.

An outspoken and influential speaker on issues of justice, peace, equal rights, human dignity, and environmental integrity, she was a member of Hashomer Hatzair, a socialist Zionist organization; she cofounded Women's Strike for Peace (1961), which lobbied against nuclear testing; she was the first congresswoman ever elected on a platform of women's rights; she initiated the Congressional Caucus on Women's Issues; she was a leader at the first UN Decade of Women Conference (1975) and the two followup conferences; she was named one of the 20 most influential women in the world in a 1977 Gallup Poll mentioned in *US News & World Report*; and she cofounded and led the Women's Environmental and Development Organization in 1990.

After a full life of leadership and fervent activism, she died on March 31, 1998.

◯ meet Ruth Bader Ginsburg

Ruth Joan Bader Ginsburg became only the second female justice of the Supreme Court upon her appointment by President Clinton in 1993. Working for a public agency as a young married woman, Ruth was demoted for becoming pregnant. In 1958, she attended Harvard Law School, despite their disdainful attitude toward women and Jews. (The dean of her law school asked her, and each of the 8 women of a class of 500, "How do you justify taking a spot from a qualified man?") Ruth became the first woman to be appointed to the *Harvard Law Review*, and she graduated first in her class—but was still turned down as clerk to a Supreme Court justice because of her gender. At her first teaching job as a professor at Rutgers Law School, Ginsburg was paid less than her male colleagues because "she had a husband with a good-paying job."

During her career as a lawyer, Justice Ginsburg advocated for women's rights and was general counsel to the American Civil Liberties Union, for which she argued six landmark cases on gender equality before the Supreme Court. She has been a fervent supporter of equal rights for all people and has always believed the law should be gender-blind.

As a Supreme Court justice, Ginsburg has been called a bold and much-needed voice for women and minorities. In her more than 20 years on the bench, she has been a consistent advocate for liberal causes and a fierce voice of dissent on the court, maintaining that her work on the court is about women's *and* men's liberation. In recent years, Ginsburg has become a cultural icon known as "the Notorious RBG," after the book of the same name. Her face adorns T-shirts, her life has been set to an opera, and her legacy has been summarized by a poster of Ginsburg that reads, "You Can't Tell Truth—Without Ruth."

◖meet Mayim Bialik

From her role as Sheldon Cooper's geeky girlfriend, Amy Farrah Fowler, on the enormously popular TV sitcom, *The Big Bang Theory*, Mayim Bialik has become a household name and a powerful moral voice in Hollywood. Bialik began her career with many small parts in TV and film in the 1980s, then starred as Blossom in the NBC TV series of the same name. The award-winning performer balanced her acting career with a solid education, receiving a B.S. in neuroscience with minors in Hebrew and Jewish studies. Unusually brainy among the Hollywood set, Bialik earned a Ph.D. in neuroscience from UCLA while continuing a passion for Jewish learning. She was raised as a Reform Jew, but moved toward Orthodoxy as she continued studying.

Bialik is a Hollywood hybrid with a strong moral compass and ready voice on issues she sees as significant. She doesn't shy away from conflict either, offering cogent thinking and vocal support for issues she values. She is a staunch Zionist, a hands-on mom to her two sons, and a very visible symbol of modern Orthodoxy. She has co-authored two books, one on parenting and the other a vegan cookbook. She also maintains a strong media presence with her website, GrokNation.com, using social media to reflect and speak out on her favorite issues: religion, parenting, pop culture, feminism, and Hollywood.

In addition to performing, Bialik writes articles, studies Torah in *chevruta* (from the Hebrew *chaver*, meaning with a partner or friend–חבר, חברותא), participates actively in Jewish organizations that support the ethical treatment of animals, while actively and publicly supporting the State of Israel. Not the ubiquitous pretty face that glams it up on the red carpet, her quirky looks and intellectual proclivities distinguish her as a high impact cultural leader in the orbits of entertainment, Judaism, and the media.

Final Words

Save the whales, save the rain forest, end illiteracy, feed 500,000 starving children—save me!

There are many causes to fight for in this world, and it can be overwhelming to decide which poster to hang up, which company to boycott, whom to support in a presidential election, and where to channel your remaining energy. Sometimes, we are pulled in so many different directions that we don't even remember what matters most.

Tikkun olam seems like a pretty big job. However, *tikkun olam* also includes helping your sibling with homework, making sure a frail older person crosses the road safely, and recycling.

As a Jewish adult, you are going to be held responsible for your actions. More will be expected of you. One of the responsibilities you will undertake is care and concern for your fellow human beings. When someone is in need of help and you are able to provide it, you extend yourself to do so. You are now going to be responsible for making the world a better place in which to live. That doesn't mean it's up to you to put a stop to nuclear weapons all on your own. It means that you are responsible for looking for opportunities to make someone's day brighter, be of assistance to someone in need, prevent others from getting hurt, and protecting the environment as best you can.

Just as in so many other difficult challenges you might be facing, Judaism has some ideas that can be useful as you consider trying to change the world. The three ideas are balance, balance, and balance.

Balance 1: It is not your responsibility to complete a task of *tikkun olam*—feeding *all* the hungry, housing *all* the homeless—but it is your responsibility to try to do something useful. Instead of demanding the impossible of you, Judaism suggests that you should actively try to help repair the world by doing what is reasonable. That takes you off the hook of too much responsibility.

Balance 2: In the whole sea of issues you could get involved in, you should strive for balance between causes that are specific to Jews and Jewish communities and causes that are not specifically Jewish. For example, you could volunteer in your local public library to reshelve books or read to children, and, at the same time, you could volunteer to be a teacher's aide in a Jewish Sunday school. Or you could learn about steps you could take to save the rain forests, while at the same time you could learn about the work of Leket, an Israeli nonprofit that collects surplus food and distributes it to Israel's needy. You'll probably find that the knowledge and experience you gain from working to further one cause will help you with the other.

Balance 3: Find a balance between doing things for yourself and doing things for others. Judaism's teachings do not encourage us to withdraw from the world, to be unhappy, or to intentionally cause ourselves to suffer. Judaism wants you to be happy and be good to yourself. It also wants you to participate actively in this world and pay attention to other people's unhappiness. As it turns out, many times *when you do things to make others happy, it makes you happy as well.*

Remember, a single act of kindness or improvement can repair the world. *Tikkun olam* is based on action. When your clothes are lying around your room, fold them and put them away. When the milk is gone, buy more. If the garbage bag is full, even though you hate to take it out, do so. *Tikkun olam* is not just about world problems, it can also be about restoring order in your own life. If everyone returned belongings to their owners, kept his or her room tidy, and offered a helping hand when there was a need, the world would be a much better place.

Your
Bat Mitzvah Gift

Dear JGirl,

If you are pre–bat mitzvah, imagine this. If you are post–bat mitzvah, remember?

In the months leading up to your bat mitzvah, there are so many preparations, so many details to arrange. You are at the center of it all—and you feel excited, special, perhaps even a little nervous. You may be working hard on learning your Haftarah or Torah portion with a teacher. You're probably preparing a speech or d'var Torah. Your extended family may be joining you from different parts of the country or the world. Your friends can't wait to celebrate with you. You and your parents are very focused on making the big day both special and meaningful. Even people who aren't Jewish know that bat mitzvah is a very big deal in the life of a Jewish girl.

And the gifts! You will receive many gifts. Even if you ask that people donate to a charity in place of giving you something, you will receive gifts. Electronics? Money? Clothes? A trip? Books? What do you imagine will be the best gift you receive? You may be surprised to learn that it's something you can't buy with money. It's simply the most valuable, the best, most enduring present—something you will treasure for the rest of your life and pass on to your children. Can you guess?

Your gift is "one adult membership in the Jewish People," a nation as old as the alphabet and as young as the nanotech bursting forth from the start-up nation of Israel. You are one among a special group, a chosen few among the families of the earth, bound by a shared history and common values. Wherever you go, you will find other members of this illustrious family that cares for you already. *Kol Yisrael arevim zeh bazeh!* Everyone among the nation of Israel is responsible one for another. No matter how far you wander, no matter how lost you may feel, you will always be welcome at home, in the Land of Israel, among the Jewish people.

At the bat mitzvah ceremony, traditional Jewish parents recite the *Barukh Sheptarani* prayer from *Genesis Rabbah* 63:10. They will say, "Blessed is He who has now freed me from the responsibility of this child." No, they are not abdicating—they'll still be your parents. But they will recognize that you are now an adult in the eyes of the Jewish people, responsible for your own behavior and ritual observance. You are now an independent citizen of the Jewish nation and your Jewish life is now yours to build.

BTW, it will take years for you to fully unwrap your gift, so we thought we'd preview a few of the highlights.

First of all, you get **the Torah**

… and a lifetime of opportunity to integrate it into your life. It's both an ancient treasure and a modern phenom. Get a copy and keep it with you wherever you go. You have thousands of years of commentary to guide you, so you can't get lost. Keep up with the weekly *parasha*. Get a *chevruta* partner. Read online commentary. Check in weekly for the story of your people. Enjoy its poetry, its mind-bending wisdom. "Turn it, and turn it, for everything is in it. Reflect on it and grow old and gray with it. Don't turn from it, for nothing is better than it" (Ben Bag Bag in *Pirkei Avot* 5:6).

You also get **an Identity** and **a People**

Within your DNA is that of the ancient Israelites, a people whose mission is to be a "light among the nations," a special, holy people. Exiled and then scattered among the nations of the world, we retained an extraordinary spirit, surviving brutal times and moving forward to producing a thriving, vibrant culture. Jews have excelled in every field of accomplishment, religious and secular. And their collected wisdom and ways of life are here for you to explore and enjoy. You are heir to an extraordinary past, an exciting present, and an amazing future. Wherever you go, you are part of a huge extended family, the Jewish People, and we welcome you with open arms!

Can you believe you also get **a Country!?!**

With the popularity of Birthright, you may even get a free trip to our homeland, the State of Israel. It's an amazing amalgam of ancient and modern, Jerusalem and Tel Aviv. As one returning teenager described the place, "Israel is the Jewish Disneyland." There are so many amazing people, places, and opportunities in Israel—and it is always there for you whether as a place of refuge or fun. Learn about your country, visit it, make friends with the Israelis you meet. And be proud of the word *Zionist*—which means you believe in survival of the Jewish people in their ancient and eternal homeland. *Am Yisrael chai!* (עם ישראל חי!)

Maybe you don't speak it, yet—but you've got **your own Language.**

Hebrew is the eternal language of the Jewish people and is spoken by more than ten million people worldwide. It is said that reading the Bible in English is like kissing a bride though her veil—because Hebrew is the vessel, the actual container, in which Jewish life percolates and lives organically. Whether it's the holy language, the Torah and its commentaries, or the cool jive of Ben Yehuda Street in Tel Aviv, every word of Hebrew you add to your vocabulary is a journey into the Jewish soul. *Be'emet!* (באמת!—Truly!)

◗ And of course, you have the solidarity **of Sisterhood.**

As a descendent of Sarah, Rebecca, Rachel, and Leah, or a convert into this lineage, you are heir to the herstory of some fabulous women. Strength, bravery, insight, wisdom, honor, and holiness are qualities owned by thousands of women in our Jewish tradition. Will you learn about these personalities? Will you take Jewish female role models? Will you accept the power and responsibility of carving out and living an exemplary Jewish life? Will you learn Torah—and teach it to your children? Until recently, many Jewish women did not learn or become rabbis. But now the world is filled with Jewish learning and leadership opportunities for all genders. Will you take your place in the worldwide sisterhood of Jewish women and light a path for the future of our people? We hope so!

The teen years can be very exciting for a young Jew like yourself. You will attend other B'nai Mitzvah rituals and parties and have the opportunity to interact with other Jewish teens, whether at camp, in Jewish learning, in the traditional Birthright trip to the State of Israel, or just as friends.

What kind of Jewish person will you become? And what will be the ways you construct your Jewish identity? Will you be traditional? Will you learn Torah and go to services? Will you become a secular Jew, attuned to the mitzvot governing behavior between one person and another? Will you learn Hebrew or become an ardent supporter of Israel? Time will tell.

Mazal Tov (מזל טוב) on your acceptance into the Nation of Israel! May you go from strength to strength!

Shalom Rav,
Ellen & the JGirl's Team

Glossary

Adonai: Often used to stand in for the name of God, Y-H-V-H, which, according to Jewish teachings, may not be pronounced.

Betzelem Elohim: "In the image of God."

Brit: Covenant, the agreement or "deal" between God and the Jewish people; also, circumcision of male Jews and the celebration associated with that ritual.

G'milut chasadim: "Acts of lovingkindness," showing care and concern for other people.

Hakhnasat orchim: "Welcoming guests."

Kavod habriot: "Honoring all creation."

Kashrut: The traditional Jewish laws and instructions about preparing and eating food.

K'doshim tihyu: "You shall be holy." God instructed the Jewish people to be holy in imitation of the Divine.

K'dushah: "Holiness"; literally means "separation."

Kibud av va'em: "Honoring father and mother."

Kol k'vodah bat melekh p'nimah: "The true majesty of a royal daughter is inside her."

Kol Israel areivim zeh bazeh: "All of Israel are responsible for one another."

Ma'akhil re'eyvim: "Feeding the hungry."

Maimonides: Rabbi Moses ben Maimon, also called Rambam, lived from 1135 to 1204. He was born in Spain and later moved to Egypt because Jews were being persecuted in Spain. He was the sultan's physician as well as a Jewish philosopher. One of the greatest Jewish scholars, he is the author of the *Guide for the Perplexed* and *Mishneh Torah,* among other works.

Menschlikhkeit: (Yiddish) the quality of being a *mensch,* a moral person who strives to behave properly and treat other people with kindness.

Midrash: Commentary on the Torah that includes creative explanations and stories. The main book of collected *Midrash* is called *Midrash Rabbah.* The word *midrash* is also used to refer to a particular tale or story.

Mikvah: A ritual bath used by both men and women separately for spiritual purification.

Mitzvah (pl. *mitzvot*): A commandment, a law, an element of instruction, or a good deed.

Pikuach nefesh: "Saving a life."

Rashi: Rabbi Shlomo Yitzchaki. One of the most important Bible scholars, he lived from 1040 to 1105 and wrote hundreds of commentaries on the Torah. Rashi made Torah learning more accessible to people who were less educated by offering simple yet insightful explanations.

Rosh Chodesh: "The head of the month." The first of each Hebrew month is a semi-festival on which special blessings are said. It is has a particularly strong connection with Jewish women who "received" the new moon festival as a reward for their faith and refusal to join in making the golden calf.

Shmirat halashon: "Guarding your tongue"; the commandment to refrain from gossip, spreading rumors, and speaking negatively about others.

Shmirat Shabbat: Observance of the Sabbath, the seventh day of the week, as a day of rest. A person who observes the Sabbath according to traditional practices is called *shomer Shabbat.*

Shutafey l'ma'aseh bereishit: Being "partners in creation" with God.

T'shuvah: The principle of "turning," to repent and correct our mistakes and wrongdoings.

Tikkun olam: "Repairing the world"; the mitzvah of looking for ways to improve, or fix the problems of, the world.

Tzedakah: Literally, "righteousness"; commonly refers to giving charity.

Tzniut: "Dignity through modesty." This includes the way we dress, eat, speak, and interact with others.

About the Jewish Religious Movements

A generation ago, many large and carefully designed temples dotted the Jewish landscape, marking the synagogue, the religious center, as the central gathering place of Jewish life. Theoretically and practically, American Jews were almost neatly contained in four religious denominations. In terms of interpreting Jewish law, Reform Judaism stood at the liberal end, followed by Reconstructionist, Conservative, and Orthodox (both modern and traditional Orthodox and including several fundamentalist groups such as the Hasidim and the Haredim).

Reform Judaism, which began in the early 19th century in Germany, regards Judaism as an ongoing process resulting from the relationship between God and the Jewish People over its history. It considers the Torah divinely inspired and open to individual interpretation based on study, and emphasizes the ethical and moral messages of the prophets to help create a just society.

Reconstructionism, founded in the 1930s, is the most recent of the major Jewish movements. Here, the essence of Judaism is defined as embodying an entire civilization, not only a religion. At the core of this civilization is a people who have the responsibility to "reconstruct" its contents from generation to generation. It's founder, Rabbi Mordecai Kaplan, also created the first American Bat Mitzvah for his daughter, Judith, in 1922.

Conservative Judaism began in the mid-19th century as a reaction to what its founders perceived to be Reform's radicalism.

It teaches that while the Torah as a whole is binding and its law remains authoritative, nonetheless new ideas and practices have always influenced Jewish beliefs. Therefore, rabbinic law and rituals may be reinterpreted and modified by *halakhic* experts.

Orthodox Judaism teaches that the Torah was divinely revealed to Moses at Mount Sinai and that the *halakhah*, the interpretive process of that law, is both divinely guided and authoritative. Thus, no law stemming from the Torah can be tampered with even if it displeases modern sensibilities. Orthodoxy often rejects more modern forms of Judaism as deviations from divine truths and authentic modes of Jewish life.

While these four continue to be the recognized major movements of Judaism, other shoots have grown from their vines. **Jewish Renewal** is a more recent movement, which draws from mysticism and meditation, seeking the reinvigoration of Jewish spiritual life. With the growth of **Chabad** communities springing up and welcoming thousands of Jewish youth across the globe, many people have come back to observe mitzvoth like Shabbat and Kashrut, calling themselves, *Ba'alei Teshuva,* those who have returned (to their religious roots).

Under the influence of feminism and the search for more meaningful Jewish expression, many have left the organized synagogue scene entirely and started independent **Minyanim**, some **Egalitarian**, meeting in homes and community centers to worship among like-minded Jews. And then there are those without specific Jewish moorings—the fastest growing population of Jews in America—who are not affiliated with synagogues.

The future of Judaism in the United States has yet to be lived, let alone transcribed—and it is your generation that will determine what lies ahead. For now, if you are curious, check out the varieties of Jewish expression in your neighborhood. You may want to spend some shabbatot visiting local synagogues. You may even want to join a youth group where, along with other teens, you can grow, invent, and cultivate your Jewish life.

The following is a listing of some popular national and international Jewish youth groups.

NFTY—North American Federation of Temple Youth / Reform (https://nfty.org)

USY—United Synagogue Youth/ Conservative (http://usy.org)

NCSY—National Conference of Synagogue Youth / Orthodox (https://ncsy.org)

BBYO—B'nai Brith Youth Organization / Pluralistic Jewish youth movement (http://bbyo.org/azabbg/about_aza_and_bbg/)

YJ—Young Judaea / oldest Zionist youth movement in the US (https://www.youngjudaea.org)

BNEI AKIVA—International Religious Zionist Youth Movement (https://www.bneiakiva.org)

RESOURCES

BOOKS to read—WEBSITES to visit

MITZVOT

Bradley Artson, *It's a Mitzvah: Step-by-Step Jewish Living*, Behrman House, 1995.

Chafetz Chaim, *The Concise Book of Mitzvot: The Commandments Which Can Be Observed Today*, Feldheim, 1990.

Linda Cohen, *1,000 Mitzvahs: How Small Acts of Kindness Can Heal, Inspire, and Change Your Life*, Seal Press, 2011.

Edward Feinstein, *Tough Questions Jews Ask: A Young Adult's Guide to Building a Jewish Life*, Jewish Lights, 2012.

Blu Greenberg, *How to Run a Traditional Jewish Household*, Simon & Schuster, 2003.

Goldie Milgram and Ellen Frankel, *Mitzvah Stories: Seeds for Inspiration and Learning, Reclaiming Judaism*, 2011.

Jewish Virtual Library (http://www.jewishvirtuallibrary.org)—An online library with excellent search function for anything you want to know about Judaism and Mitzvot.

BLESSINGS

Marcia Falk, *The Book of Blessings: New Jewish Prayers for Daily Life, The Sabbath,* and the *New Moon Festival,* CCAR Press, 2017.

Irwin Kula and Vanessa Ochs, *The Book of Jewish Sacred Practices: CLAL's Guide to Everyday and Holiday Rituals and Blessings*, Jewish Lights, 2002

Aliza Lavie, *A Jewish Women's Prayer Book*, Spiegel & Graus, 2008.

Rav Noson of Breslov, *Between Me and You: Heartfelt Prayers for Each Jewish Woman*, Nachas Books, 2012.

Siddur Interlinear (translation) Sabbath and Festival Prayers—Schottenstein Edition, 2002.

Siddur Audio (http://www.sidduraudio.com/index.html)—Learn how to "daven" from this site which offers traditional chanting of classic Jewish prayers.

JEWISH IDENTITY

Sandy Asher, ed. *With All my Heart, With All My Mind: Stories About Growing Up Jewish*, Simon and Schuster, 2000.

Arthur Green, *These Are the Words: A Vocabulary of Jewish Spiritual Life*, Jewish Lights, 2014.

Lawrence Kushner, *The Book of Miracles: A Young Person's Guide to Jewish Spiritual Awareness*, Jewish Lights, Learn How You Want, 2016.

Stan Mack, *The Story of the Jews: A 4,000-Year Adventure—A Graphic History Book*, Jewish

Lights, 2006.

Judea and Ruth Pearl, *I am Jewish: Personal Reflections Inspired by the Last Words of Daniel Pearl*, Jewish Lights, 2004

Joseph Telushkin, *Jewish Literacy: The Most Important Things to Know About the Jewish Religion, Its People, and its History*, William Morrow, 2008.

David J. Wolpe, Why Be Jewish?, Holt Paperbacks, 1995

My Jewish Learning (https://www.myjewishlearning.com)— Advertised as "The Premiere site for all things Jewish." Huge go-to site addressing most questions you might have about Judaism.

YourJStory (http://www.yourjstory.com) is a site by and for Jewish millenials celebrating the diversity of Jewish experience— *one people. many stories.*—and the fun of being Jewish.

BAT MITZVAH

Paula Friedman, *My Basmati Bat Mitzvah*, Amulet Books, 2013.

Amy Kurzweil, *Flying Couch: A Graphic Memoir, Black Balloon Publishing*, 2016.

Goldie Milgram, *Reclaiming Bar/Bat Mitzvah as a Spiritual Rite of Passage*, Reclaiming Judaism Press, 2014.

Jeffrey Salkin, *For Kids—Putting God on the Guest List: How to Claim the Spiritual Meaning of your Bar or Bat Mitzvah*, Jewish Lights, 2007.

Barbara Vinick & Shulamit Reinharz, *Today I am a Woman: Stories of Bat Mitzvah around the World*, Indiana U. Press, 2011.

Elizabeth Suneby and Diane Heiman, *The Mitzvah Project Book: Making Mitzvah Part of your Bar/Bat Mitzvah ... and Your Life*, Jewish Lights, 2011

JEWISH WOMEN

Lisa Aiken, *To Be a Jewish Woman*, Createspace, 2016.

Deborah Bodin Cohen, *Lilith's Ark: Teenage Tales of Biblical Women*, Jewish Publication Society, 2006.

Anne Frank, *The Diary of a Young Girl*, Bantam, 1993.

Etty Hillesum, *An Interrupted Life: The Diaries of Etty Hillesum*, Pantheon Books, 1996.

Charlotte Salomon, *Life? Or Theatre?*, Overlook Press, 2017.

Shiela F. Segal, *Women of Valor- Stories of Great Jewish Women who Helped Shape the Twentieth Century*, Behrman House, 1996.

Elinor and Robert Slater, *Great Jewish Women*, Jonathan David, 2015.

Hannah Volavkova, editor, *I Never Saw Another Butterfly: Children's Drawings and Poems from the Terrezin Concentration Camp, 1942–1944*, Schocken, 1994.

Irin Varmon and Shana Knizhik, *Notorious RGB: The Life and Times of Ruth Bader Ginsberg*, Dey Street Books, 2015.

Jewish Women's Archive (https://jwa.org) lots of info about and writing from Jewish women throughout history.

EATING

Jacob Attias, *The JEWLISH Cookbook: 175 Pages of Fun, Easy, and Authentic Jewish Recipes*, Jewlish, 2017.

Susie Fishbein, *Kosher by Design: Teens and 20-Somethings*, Mesorah Publications, 2010.

Rena Rossner, *Eating the Bible: Over 50 Delicious Recipes to Feed Your Body and Nourish Your Soul*, Skyhorse Publishing, 2013.

Freda Reider, *The Hallah Book: Recipes, History, and Traditions*, Ktav, 1986.

The Joy of Kosher, (https://www.joyofkosher.com), described as the Jewish Rachel Ray, Jamie Geller hosts a site with thousands of recipes and youtube videos.

National Eating Disorders Association (https://www.nationaleating-disorders.org/eating-disorders-jewish-community)—with a special page on eating disorders in the Jewish community and a helpline you can call.

JEWISH LIFE CYCLE

Yosef I. Abramowitz and Susan Silverman, *Jewish Family & Life: Traditions, Holidays, and Values*, St. Martin's Press, 1998.

Matt Axelrod, *Your Guide to the Jewish Holidays*, Jason Aronson, 2014.

Goldie Milgram, *Living Jewish Life Cycle: How to Create Meaningful Rites of Passage at Every Stage of Life*, Jewish Lights 2008.

Abby Pogrebin, *My Jewish Year: 18 Holidays, One Wondering Jew*, Fig Tree Books, 2017.

Moving Traditions (https://www.movingtraditions.org/perspectives-from-teens/)—Foundation that facilitates popular rosh hodesh groups across America.

TORAH STUDY

Hayim Nachman Bialik and Yehoshua Ravnitsky, eds., *The Book of Legends/Sefer Ha-Aggadah*, Schocken Books, 1992.

The Chumash/The Torah, Stone Edition (Artscroll, English and Hebrew), 1993.

Ellen Frankel, *The Five Books of Miriam*, Harper Collins, 1997.

Elyse Goldstein, ed., *The Women's Torah Commentary: New Insights from Women Rabbis on the 54 Weekly Torah Portions*, Jewish Lights, 2000. -

Elyse Goldstein, ed., *The Women's Haftarah Commentary: New Insights from Women Rabbis on the 54 Weekly Haftarah Portions, the 5 Megillot, and Special Shabbatot*, Jewish Lights, 2000.

Jeffrey Salkin, *Text Messages: A Torah Commentary for Teens*, Jewish Lights, 2012.

My Jewish Learning (https://www.myjewishlearning.com) is a one-stop-shop for most Jewish questions and study, but the Jewish Web is rich in Torah-study sites, as well. A brief few include:

http://www.aish.com—Self-advertised as "Everything Jewish"

https://www.bimbam.com—Torah videos and apps

http://www.chabad.org/parshah—Parsha study and more

http://www.webyeshiva.org—Torah lectures and classes

Sefaria (https://www.sefaria.org)—Ginormous and free online library of classic Jewish texts in Hebrew and English.

HEBREW

Eliezer Ben-Yehuda, *Fulfillment of Prophecy: The Life of Eliezer Ben-Yehuda*, Booksurge Publishing, 2009.

Lawrence Kushner, *The Book of Hebrew Letters: A Mystical Alphabet*, Jewish Lights, 1990.

Evelyn Simon and Joseph Anderson, *Teach Yourself to Read Hebrew*, EKS Publishing, 2008.

Online Hebrew Learning (http://learninghebrew.net/top-10-methods-to-learn-hebrew-online/) listing of several Hebrew learning sites and approaches.

YOUR CHANGING BODY

Ruth Bell, ed. *Changing Bodies, Changing Lives: A Book for Teens on Sex and Relationships,* Random House, 1998.

Joan Jacobs Brumberg, *The Body Project: An Intimate History of American Girls,* Random House, 1998.

Bryan Lask and Lucy Watson, *Can I Tell you about Eating Disorders?: A Guide for Friends, Family, and Professionals,* Jessica Kingsley Publishers, 2014.

Gila Manolson, *Inside, Outside: A Fresh Look at Tzniut,* Targum Press, 2005.

Valorie Schafer, *The Care and Keeping of You: The Body Book for Girls,* American Girl, 1998).

Girls Health (https://www.girlshealth.gov)—a website sponsored by the U.S. Department of Human Services.

STAYING HEALTHY

Mayim Bialik, *Girling Up: How to be Strong, Smart, and Spectacular,* Philomel Books, 2017.

Diane Bloomfield, *Torah Yoga: Experiencing Jewish Wisdom through Classic Postures,* Josey Bass, 2004.

Sean Covey, *The 7 Habits of Highly Effective Teens,* Touchstone, 2014.

Mary Pipher, *Reviving Ophelia: Saving the Selves of Adolescent Girls,* Ballantine Books, 2002.

Daniel Polish, Daniel B. Syme, and Bernard Zlotowitz, *Drugs, Sex, and Integrity: What Does Judaism Say?,* URJ Press, 1991.

Sarah Shandler, *Ophelia Speaks: Adolescent Girls Write about Their Search for Self,* Perennial, 1999.

Planned Parenthood (https://www.plannedparenthood.org/learn/teens)—information about relationships, sex, and your body.

SHABBAT

Abraham Joshua Heschel, *The Sabbath*, Farrar Straus Giroux, 2005.

Moshe Mykoff, *Seventh Heaven: Shabbat with Rebbe Nachman of Breslov*, Jewish Lights, 2003.

Mark Dov Shapiro, *Gates of Shabbat: A Guide for Observing Shabbat*, CCAR Press, 2016.

Judith Shulevitz, *The Sabbath World: Glimpses of a Different Order of Time*, Random House, 2011.

Ron Wolfson. *Shabbat: The Family Guide for Observing Shabbat*, Jewish Lights, 2002.

Shabbat (http://www.chabad.org/library/article_cdo/aid/253215/jewish/Shabbat.htm) Chabad site is rich in resources for experiencing a traditional Shabbat.

ISRAEL

Daniel Gordis, *Israel: A Concise History of a Nation Reborn*, Ecco, 2017

Yossi Klein HaLevi, *Like Dreamers: The Story of the Israeli Paratroopers Who Reunited Jerusalem and Divided a Nation*, Harper, 2014.

Dan Senor and Saul Singer, *Start-Up Nation: The Story of Israel's Economic Miracle*, Twelve, 2011.

Leon Uris, *Exodus*, Bantam, 1983

Yigal Yadin, *Masada*, Random House, 1966.

The David Project (https://www.davidproject.org)—Student Israel Advocacy Group.

Women of the Wall (http://www.womenofthewall.org.il)—Egalitarian organization striving for women's religious rights at the Western Wall/ The Kotel.

Birthright Israel (https://www.birthrightisrael.com//)—Organization that funds free trips to Israel for Jewish teens.

Notes

Chapter One (pp. 1–16)

I do not know what's wrong: Excerpted from the November 26, 1890, entry in the diary of Jennie Franklin (American Jewish Archives, MS 502).

Chapter Two (pp. 17–33)

For poor brides who were: This poem by Kadya Molodowsky, "Women-Poems, VI," appears in *Paper Bridges: Selected Poems of Kadya Molodowsky*, edited and translated by Kathryn Hellerstein (Detroit: Wayne State University Press, 1999), 79.

Chapter Three (pp. 35–55)

The dishes of my aunt Latifa and her cook Nessim: This excerpt was taken from *The Book of Jewish Food: An Odyssey from Samarkand to New York* by Claudia Roden (New York: Alfred A. Knopf, 1996), 569.

Invite people living in your community who: These activities are excerpted from *Jewish Family & Life: Traditions, Holidays, and Values for Today's Parents and Children* by Yosef Abramowitz and Susan Silverman (New York: Golden Guides from St. Martin's Press, 1998), 124.

It wasn't about dishes, or law: This excerpt was taken from *Miriam's Kitchen* by Elizabeth Ehrlich (New York: Viking, 1997), 127.

My mother grew up in a very religious home: This quotation by Karen Erdos is from Ellen Umansky and Dianne Ashton's *Four Centuries of Jewish Women's Spirituality* (Boston: Beacon Press, 1992), 308.

Before I respond to the growl in my stomach: This quotation comes from *Jewish Family & Life: Traditions, Holidays, and Values for Today's Parents and Children* by Yosef Abramowitz and Susan Silverman (New York: Golden Guides from St. Martin's Press, 1998), 124.

An eating disorder is not about food: This quotation from Rabbi Jennifer Rebecca Marx was cited by Rabbi Janet Marder in her sermon "All Who Are Hungry," March 31, 2004. This sermon is available online at www.betham.org/sermons/marder040331.html.

In the world of adolescent girls: This excerpt comes from *Ophelia Speaks: Adolescent Girls Write about Their Search for Self,* edited by Sarah Shandler (New York: Perennial, 1999), 12.

Chapter Four (pp. 57–76)

Set apart one day a week: This excerpt comes from *The Sabbath: Its Meaning for Modern Man,* by Abraham Joshua Heschel (New York: Farrar, Straus and Giroux, 2005), 28.

Shabbat adds a sweetness and a rhythm: This excerpt comes from *It's a Mitzvah,* by Bradley Shavit Artson (New Jersey: Berhman House, 1995), 134.

The Sabbath began: This text is reprinted from Jennie Rosenfeld Gerstley's *"Reminiscences"—of Chicago in the 1860s and 1870s* (American Jewish Archives, Box 2072).

At dusk, I kindled four candles: This poem by Kadya Molodowsky, "Sabbath Song," appears in *Paper Bridges: Selected Poems of Kadya Molodowsky,* edited and translated by Kathryn Hellerstein (Detroit: Wayne State University Press, 1999), 453 and 455.

The women gathered for prayer: This text is reprinted from Malkah Shapiro's *The Rebbe's Daughter: Memoirs of a Hasidic Girl in*

Poland before World War II (Philadelphia: Jewish Publication Society, 2001), 66.

FAQs about Shabbat: Reprinted from *Every Persons' Guide to Shabbat* by Ronald H. Isaacs (Northvale, N.J.: Jason Aronson, 1998), 103–109.

Lead prayers and Torah discussion themselves on Shabbat: For more about this movement, see *The First Jewish Catalogue* by Michael and Sharon Strassfeld (Philadelphia: Jewish Publication Society, 1976).

I met my friend Eleanor: From a personal communication from Boorstein to the authors.

Make your own braided havdalah candle: This activity, created by Rebecca E. Kotkin, is excerpted from http://jewishfamily.com /jc/holidays/havdalah_with_a.txt.

Chapter Five (pp. 77–90)

Do you know about all these Jewish female athletes?: This list is from a letter to the editor of the *Foreword* by Nancy Vineberg.

An activity entitled "Baby Steps": Based on text from *The 7 Habits of Highly Effective Teens* by Sean Covey (New York: Fireside, 1998).

Chapter Six (pp. 91–103)

According to author Gila Manolson: For more on this, see *Inside, Outside: A Fresh Look at Tzniut,* by Gila Manolson (Nanuet, N.Y.: Targum Press, 2005), 25.

With puberty, girls face: This quotation comes from *Reviving Ophelia: Saving the Selves of Adolescent Girls,* by Mary Pipher (New York: Ballantine Books, 2002), 38.

Got new hat and shoes yesterday: Excerpted from the April 19, 1896, entry in the diary of Bella Weretnikow, 17, Seattle (American Jewish Archives, MS 179).

Tues., 1 August 1944.... Excerpted from *The Diary of a Young Girl* by Anne Frank (New York: Bantam Books, 1993), 266.

Once upon a time, there was a prince: For the original story, see "The Turkey Prince" in *The Seven Beggars & Other Kabbalistic Tales of Rebbe Nachman of Breslov*, translated and with annotations by Rabbi Aryeh Kaplan; introduction by Rabbi Chaim Kramer (Woodstock, Vt.: Jewish Lights, 2005).

Chapter Seven (pp. 105–127)

Welcome to the sisterhood: This ritual has been adapted from Rabbi Goldie Milgram's "Ritual for Welcoming Bodily Change," available at www.RitualWell.org.

Rabbi Goldstein's revised version allows: This blessing initially appeared in *Lilith* (Spring 1990), 32.

When I was a freshman in college: Excerpted from *Celebrating Our Cycles: A Jewish Woman's Introduction to Menstruation and Womanhood* by Rachel Shnider (Waltham, Mass.: Hadassah-Brandeis Institute, 2002).

It makes sense to begin with: This quotation comes from *Like Bread on the Seder Plate: Jewish Lesbians and the Transformation of Tradition* by Rebecca Alpert (New York: Columbia University Press, 1997), 54.

Touching inappropriately: This list is from "Know Your Rights," *Teen Voices*, 9:2 (2000), 35.

Chapter Eight (pp. 129–144)

Gracious and merciful God: This text is quoted from *It's a Mitzvah* by Bradley Shavit Artson (Springfield, N.J.: Behrman House, 1995), 153.

Once there was a woman who said awful things about another person: This retelling is inspired by *Yettele's Feathers* by Joan Rothenberg (New York: Hyperion Paperbacks, 1996).

We abuse, we betray, we are cruel: This translation is from the New York Rabbinical Assembly *Mahzor* for Rosh Hashanah and Yom Kippur, 1972, 1978.

Suicidal Boyfriend, The story of Cyberbully Michelle Carter is based on two articles from the Boston Globe by Maria Cremer and Kevin Cullen: https://www.bostonglobe.com/metro/2017 /06/16/three-little-words-sunk-michelle-carter/7MgZibLEgQ-7As6zvNOaDJI/story.html and https://www.bostonglobe.com /metro/2017/06/16 /three-little-words-sunk-michelle-carter /7MgZibLEgQ7As6zvNOaDJI/story.html

Chapter Nine (pp. 145–164)

It was young Jewish women in their teens: This text was written by Michele Landsberg, columnist for the *Toronto Star.* It appeared on March 8, 1997.

I was reared in a traditional Jewish household: This quote comes from "Alicia Silverstone's Most Ambitious Role Ever," an article written by Ivor Davis and available online at www.jvibe.com/ popculture/stone.shtml.

About the Jewish Religous Movements (pp. 173–174)

There are now four major Jewish religious movements: This text comes from *How to Be a Perfect Stranger, 3rd Edition: The Essential Religious Etiquette Handbook* (Woodstock, Vt.: SkyLight Paths, 2002), 133.

CPSIA information can be obtained
at www.ICGtesting.com
Printed in the USA
BVOW08s1527101117
500072BV00003B/498/P